DEBBIE
MUMM®

Joy Joy Joy

DEBBIE
MUMM

Dear Friends,

The holidays can be the most joyous time of year when you share your loving and generous spirit with family and friends. Handmade gifts, homemade food, and beautiful decor creatively crafted by you are all wonderful ways to spread cheer and make special memories for loved ones.

I chose four favorite themes that are close to my heart—home, friendship, nature, and whimsy—to focus on for this holiday book. My team and I loved creating easy-to-do projects and crafts along with quilts and decor for all of these themes. What better way to share yourself, honor tradition, and make new memories than with the gift of something handmade by you?

A quilt makes a beautiful backdrop for a family photograph or to hang over the mantel for the entire season. Reinvent a side table with a table runner and grace your dining room with a new centerpiece. Before the gifts appear, a new tree skirt will bring color and pizazz to "the tree." A banner that declares "JOY" on the front door shows all who pass by that the holiday spirit is alive and well in your home.

Your family and your friends will be touched by the many ways you use your creativity to express your love and to make the holiday special and joyous for all. With a cup of peppermint cocoa and a ginger cookie to set the mood, enjoy looking through this book and begin planning for a most memorable and special Christmas season.

START SPREADING THE JOY!
Debbie Mumm

TABLE OF
Contents

WILDBERRY LODGE

JINGLE JOYS

SNOW FRIENDS

HOLIDAY HOMES

ET CETERA

Wildberry LODGE

A Natural Christmas ~ Nature's abundance and beauty are celebrated in this group of quilting and decorating projects.

A bed size quilt, a beautiful botanical table setting, and many more projects bring nature's beauty indoors for a holiday full of wilderness charm.

MOOSE CROSSING
Bed Quilt

Read all instructions before beginning and use ¼"-wide seam allowance throughout. Read Cutting Strips and Pieces on page 92 prior to cutting fabric.

GETTING STARTED

This quilt consists of two quick-to-make blocks each measuring 16½" square unfinished. It is further enhanced with pieced and regular borders. Refer to Accurate Seam Allowance on page 92. Whenever possible use the Assembly Line Method on page 92. Press seams in the direction of arrows.

Tip: Use a two-tone striped fabric for leaf appliqués to add depth and dimension.

MAKING THE BERRY BLOCK

1. Sew one 4½" x 42" Fabric C strip to one 4½" x 42" Fabric D strip lengthwise to make a strip set. Press seam toward Fabric C. Make three. Cut strip set into twenty-four 4½"-wide segments as shown.

4½

Make 3 strip sets
Cut 24 segments

Moose Crossing Bed Quilt Finished Size: 81" x 97"	FIRST CUT		SECOND CUT	
	Number of Strips or Pieces	Dimensions	Number of Pieces	Dimensions
Fabric A Moose Background and Second Border Accents 2⅛ yards	3 5	16½" x 42" 4½" x 42"	6	16½" squares
Fabric B Berry Block Background ⅞ yard	3	8½" x 42"	12	8½" squares
Fabric C Block, Second and Outside Borders Accents 2½ yards	19	4½" x 42" (8 strips used for strip sets)	84	4½" squares
Fabric D Block and Outside Border Accents 1¾ yards	13	4½" x 42" (3 strips used for strip sets)	40	4½" x 8½"
Fabric E Block Sashing ⅔ yard	14	1½" x 42"	8	1½" x 16½"
Fabric F Moose Block Accents 1½ yards	6	8½" x 42"	24	8½" squares
BORDERS				
First Border ½ yard	4 3	2½" x 42" 2" x 42"		
Third and Fifth Borders ⅞ yard	8 8	2" x 42" 1½" x 42"		
Fourth Border ½ yard	8	2" x 42"		
Binding ⅞ yard	10	2¾" x 42"		

Backing - 7⅜ yards

Batting - 88" x 104"

Lightweight Fusible Web - 1½ yards

Moose Appliqués - ½ yard

Leaf and Stem Appliqués - ½ yard

Berry Appliqués - ⅛ yard

2. Sew two units from step 1 as shown. Press. Sew this unit to one 8½" Fabric B square together as shown. Press. Make twelve.

Make 12

8½

8½

Make 12

3. Sew two units from step 2 together as shown. Press. Make six. Block measures 16½" square.

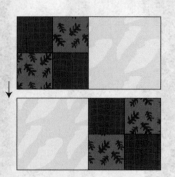

Make 6
Block measures 16½" square

4. Refer to appliqué instructions on page 93. Our instructions are for Quick-Fuse Appliqué, but if you prefer hand appliqué add ¼"-wide seam allowance. Use Berry/Leaf appliqué patterns on page 17 to trace twelve sets of leaves and berries on paper side of fusible web. Use appropriate fabrics to prepare leaf and berry appliqués for fusing.

5. Press 5¾" x 13¾" fusible web to wrong side of one 6" x 14" stem fabric piece. Cut fused fabric into six ⅜" x 13¼" strips.

The first crisp snow of winter brings a moose herd to the edge of the forest to search for food among the berries and pines. The quiet simplicity of the woods in winter is captured in this easy-to-piece bed quilt. A variety of pieced and plain borders extends the peaceful illusion to the very edges of the quilt top.

6. Referring to photo on page 7, layout on page 9, and appliqué pattern on page 17 (note placement guide) arrange and fuse stems, leaves, and berries to blocks. Finish appliqué edges with machine satin stitch or other decorative stitching as desired. **Note:** We elected not to finish the appliqué edges on the Berry Blocks; instead, during the quilting process we stitched over all raw edges to hold them in place and to prevent raveling.

MAKING THE MOOSE BLOCK

1. Refer to Quick Corner Triangles on page 92. Making quick corner triangle units, sew four 8½" Fabric F squares to one 16½" Fabric A square as shown. Press. Make six. Blocks measure 16½" square.

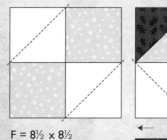

F = 8½ x 8½
A = 16½ x 16½

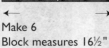

Make 6
Block measures 16½"

2. Refer to appliqué instructions on page 93. Our instructions are for Quick-Fuse Appliqué, but if you prefer hand appliqué add ¼"-wide seam allowance. Use Moose appliqué pattern on page 16 to trace three Moose and three reversed Moose, on paper side of fusible web. Use appropriate fabrics to prepare all appliqués for fusing.

3. Refer to photo on page 7 and layout on page 9 to position and fuse appliqués to block. Finish appliqué edges with machine satin stitch or other decorative stitching as desired.

ASSEMBLY THE QUILT

1. Arrange and sew together two 1½" x 16½" Fabric E strips, two Berry Blocks, and one Moose Block as shown. Press. Make two.

Make 2

2. Arrange and sew together two 1½" x 16½" Fabric E strips, two Moose Blocks, and one Berry Block as shown. Press Make two.

Make 2

3. Sew ten 1½" x 42" Fabric E strips together end-to-end to make one continuous 1½"-wide Fabric E strip. From this strip cut five 1½" x 50½" strips and two 1½" x 69½" strips.

4. Referring to photo on page 7 and layout on page 9, arrange and sew together five 1½" x 50½" Fabric E strips and rows from steps 1 and 2. Press seams toward Fabric E.

5. Sew 1½" x 69½" Fabric E strips to sides of quilt. Press.

ADDING THE BORDERS

1. Sew three 2" x 42" First Border strips together end-to-end to make one continuous 2"-wide First Border strip. Cut two 2" x 52½" First Border strips. Sew to top and bottom of quilt. Press seams toward border.

2. Sew two 2½" x 42" First Border strips together end-to-end. Make two. Cut two 2½" x 72½" First Border strips and sew to sides of quilt. Press. **Note:** Side strips are ½" wider than top and bottom First Border strips.

MOOSE CROSSING *Bed Quilt*
Finished Size: 81" x 97"

5. Sew ten segments from step 3 end-to-end alternating colors to make one 4½" x 80½" pieced strip. Press. Make two. Referring to photo on page 7 and layout, sew strips to sides of quilt. Press.

6. Sew 2"-wide Third Border strips end-to-end to make one continuous 2"-wide border strip. Measure quilt through center from side to side. Cut two Third Border strips to this measurement. Sew to top and bottom of quilt. Press seams towards border.

7. Measure quilt through center from top to bottom including borders just added. Cut two 2"-wide Third Border strips to this measurement. Sew to sides of quilt. Press.

8. Refer to steps 6 and 7 to join, measure, trim, and sew 2"-wide Fourth Border and 1½"-wide Fifth Border strips to top, bottom and sides of quilt. Press seams toward each newly added border.

9. Refer to Quick Corner Triangles on page 92. Making quick corner triangle units, sew two 4½" Fabric C squares to one 4½" x 8½" Fabric D piece as shown. Press. Make forty.

C = 4½ x 4½
D = 4½ x 8½
Make 40

3. Sew one 4½" x 42" Fabric A strip and one 4½" x 42" Fabric C strip together lengthwise to make a strip set. Press seam toward Fabric C. Make five. From strip set, cut thirty-four 4½"-wide segments as shown.

4½

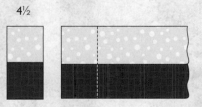

Make 5 strip sets
Cut 34 segments

4. Sew seven segments from step 3 end-to-end alternating colors to make one 4½" x 56½" pieced strip. Press. Make two. Referring to photo on page 7 and layout, sew pieced-strip to top and bottom of quilt, checking orientation of fabric prior to sewing. Press seams toward First Border.

10. Referring to photo on page 7 and layout, sew together nine units from step 9. Press. Make two. Sew to top and bottom of quilt, checking orientation of fabrics prior to sewing. Press seams toward Fifth Border.

11. Referring to photo on page 7 and layout, sew together eleven units from step 9. Press. Sew this unit between two 4½" Fabric C squares. Press. Make two. Sew units to sides of quilt. Press.

LAYERING AND FINISHING

1. Cut backing crosswise into three equal pieces. Sew pieces together lengthwise to make one 88" x 120" (approximate) backing piece. Press and trim to 88" x 104".

2. Referring to Layering the Quilt on page 94, arrange and baste backing, batting, and top together. Hand or machine quilt as desired. **Reminder:** Quilt all appliqué edges that weren't previously stitched with decorative stitches. We chose to highlight the Moose Blocks with Big Stitch Quilting. See below for instructions for this technique and photo on page 7 for placement.

3. Refer to Binding the Quilt on page 94. Sew 2¾" x 42" binding strips end-to-end to make one continuous 2¾"-wide binding strip. Bind quilt to finish.

BIG STITCH QUILTING TECHNIQUE

If you plan to combine machine quilting and the Big Stitch Technique, complete machine quilting first. To make a Big Stitch, use embroidery needle with number 8 crochet thread, perle cotton, or three strands of embroidery floss. Anchor the knot in batting as in quilting. Make ¼"-long stitches on top of quilt and ⅛"-long stitches under quilt, so large stitches stand out.

Big Stitch

Debbie's DECORATING TIPS

Nature provides an abundance of decorating materials that are perfect for holiday decorating. Pinecones are among my favorites as they come in many shapes and sizes, are interesting and textural, and can be rustic or elegant depending on how they are used.

Extend all the warmth of the great outdoors to your guests with this easy centerpiece that's perfect for a dining or entry table. A metal plate stacker is outfitted with wood bowls and filled with a variety of pinecones. Red apples, leaves, and berries add contrasting color and texture to this simple, yet effective, presentation. A candle in the top bowl adds scent and shine to this welcoming display.

Carry the theme further by welcoming dinner guests with pinecones in painted terracotta pots. Accented with stenciled checks and a handwritten name, these party favors personalize each guest's place setting.

Rounds of birch logs become candleholders with the addition of river rocks and faux berries. Many people collect rocks during their outdoor adventures and this is a great way to display your collection and bring natural warmth to your home.

See page 16 for more ideas for decorating with nature's gifts.

MOOSE CROSSING Wall Quilt

Quick GIFT IDEA!

Moose Crossing Wall Quilt Finished Size: 49" x 49"	FIRST CUT		SECOND CUT	
	Number of Strips or Pieces	Dimensions	Number of Pieces	Dimensions
Fabric A ½ yard Moose Background	1	16½" x 42"	2	16½" squares
Fabric B ⅓ yard Berry Block Background	1	8½" x 42"	4	8½" squares
Fabric C ⅙ yard Block Accent	1	4½" x 42"		
Fabric D ⅙ yard Block Accent	1	4½" x 42"		
Fabric E 1⅛ yards Block Sashing and Outside Border Accents	6 6	4½" x 42" 1½" x 42"	44 2 3 2	4½" squares 1½" x 35½" 1½" x 33½" 1½" x 16½"
Fabric F 1⅙ yards Moose Block Accent	2 5	8½" x 42" 4½" x 42"	8 20	8½" squares 4½" x 8½"
BORDERS				
First Border ⅓ yard	4	2" x 42"	2 2	2" x 38½" 2" x 35½"
Second Border ¼ yard	4	1½" x 42"	2 2	1½" x 40½" 1½" x 38½"
Binding ½ yard	5	2¾" x 42"		

Backing - 3 yards
Batting - 54" x 54"
Moose Appliqués - ¼ yard
Leaf and Stem Appliqués - ⅙ yard
Berry Appliqués - Scrap
Lightweight Fusible Web - ⅝ yard

GETTING STARTED

Bring the spirit of the great outdoors to any room by making this easy wall quilt. Read all instructions before beginning and use ¼"-wide seam allowance throughout. Read Cutting Strips and Pieces on page 92 prior to cutting fabric. Refer to Accurate Seam Allowance on page 92. Whenever possible use the Assembly Line Method on page 92. Press seams in the direction of arrows.

MAKING THE QUILT

1. Refer to Making the Berry Block pages 6-8, steps 1-6 to make two blocks. In Step 1, use one 4½" x 42" Fabric C strip and one 4½" x 42" Fabric D strip. Cut eight 4½"-wide segments from strip set. In steps 4-6 trace, fuse, and cut four sets of leaves and berries and two stems.

2. Refer to Making the Moose Block page 8, steps 1-3 to make two blocks. In steps 2-3 trace, fuse and cut two moose, one regular and one reversed. If desired, finish moose edges with satin or decorative stitching.

3. Referring to photo, sew one 1½" x 16½" Fabric E strip between one Berry Block and one Moose Block. Press seams toward Fabric E. Make two, one of each variation.

4. Referring to photo, arrange and sew together three 1½" x 33½" Fabric E strips to rows from step 3. Press toward Fabric E. Sew this unit between two 1½" x 35½" Fabric E strips. Press.

5. Sew two 2" x 35½" First Border strips to top and bottom of quilt. Press. Sew 2" x 38½" First Border strips to sides. Press.

6. Sew 1½" x 38½" Second Border strips to top and bottom of quilt. Press. Sew 1½" x 40½" Second Border strips to sides. Press.

7. Refer to Quick Corner Triangles on page 92. Making quick corner triangle units, sew two 4½" Fabric E squares to one 4½" x 8½" Fabric F piece as shown. Press. Make twenty.

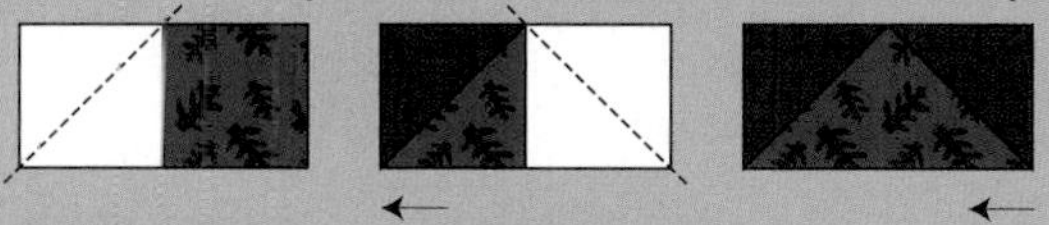

E = 4½ x 4½
F = 4½ x 8½
Make 20

8. Referring to photo, sew together five units from step 7. Press. Make four. Sew two units to top and bottom of quilt, checking orientation of fabric prior to sewing. Press.

9. Sew one unit from step 8 between two 4½" Fabric E squares. Press. Make two. Sew to sides of quilt. Press.

LAYERING AND FINISHING

1. Cut backing crosswise into two equal pieces. Sew pieces together lengthwise to make one 54" x 80" (approximate) backing piece. Press and trim to 54" x 54".

2. Referring to Layering the Quilt on page 94, arrange and baste backing, batting and top together. Hand or machine quilt as desired. **Reminder:** Quilt all appliqué edges that weren't previously stitched.

3. Refer to Binding the Quilt on page 94. Sew 2¾" x 42" binding strips end-to-end to make one continuous 2¾"-wide binding strip. Bind quilt to finish.

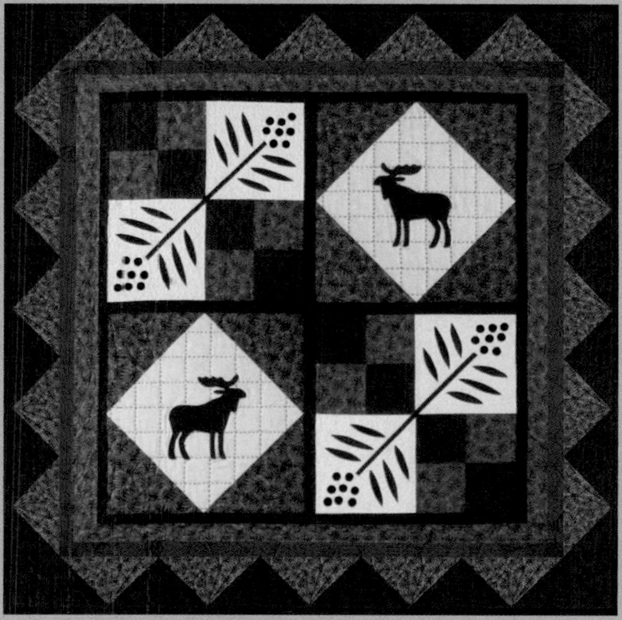

WILDBERRY Table Runner

Wildberry Table Runner Finished Size: 59½" x 20¾"	FIRST CUT		SECOND CUT	
	Number of Strips or Pieces	Dimensions	Number of Pieces	Dimensions
Fabric A Appliqué Background ¼ yard	1	6½" x 42"		
Fabric B Light Green ⅜ yard	1 1	6½" x 42" 5½" x 42"	4	5½" squares
Fabric C Block Accent Border and Two-colored Binding ½ yard	2 5	2¾" x 42" 1½" x 42"	2 6 4	1½" x 14½" 1½" x 13½" 1½" x 12½"
Fabric D Dark Green and Two-colored Binding ½ yard	3 3	2¾" x 42" 2½" x 42"	4 4	2½" x 13½" 2½" x 11½"
Fabric E Medium Green ¼ yard	2	2½" x 42"	4 4	2½" x 9½" 2½" x 7½"

Backing - 1¾ yards
Batting - 65" x 25"
Leaf and Stem Appliqués - ¼ yard
Lightweight Fusible Web - ½ yard
¾" Buttons - 12

Fabric Requirements and Cutting Instructions

Read all instructions before beginning and use ¼"-wide seam allowance throughout. Read Cutting Strips and Pieces on page 92 prior to cutting fabric.

Getting Started

Nature comes indoors to adorn your table with the rich colors of a pine forest. Clever block construction gives an intricate designer look, but blocks are easy to make. **Tip:** Use a two-tone striped fabric for leaf appliqués to add depth and dimension. Refer to Accurate Seam Allowance on page 92. Whenever possible use the Assembly Line Method on page 92. Press seams in the direction of arrows.

Making the Table Runner

1. Sew 6½" x 42" Fabric B strip and 6½" x 42" Fabric A strip together lengthwise to make a strip set. Press toward Fabric B. Cut strip set into six 6½"-wide segments as shown. Sew units together in pairs alternating colors as shown. Press. Make three.

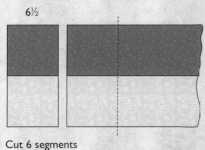

6½
Cut 6 segments
Make 3

2. Sew one 1½" x 12½" Fabric C strip to one unit from step 1 as shown. Press. Sew this unit between two 1½" x 13½" Fabric C strips as shown. Press. Make two.

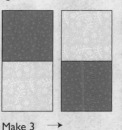

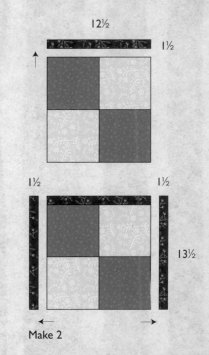

12½
1½
1½
1½
13½
Make 2

3. Sew one unit from step 1 between two 1½" x 12½" Fabric C strips. Press. Sew this unit between two 1½" x 14½" Fabric C strips as shown. Press.

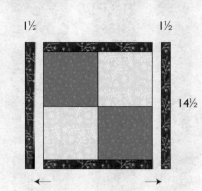

1½   1½

14½

4. Sew one 2½" x 7½" Fabric E piece to one 5½" Fabric B square as shown, note Fabric E extends past Fabric B square. Press. Sew this unit to one 2½" x 9½" Fabric E piece as shown. Press. Make four.

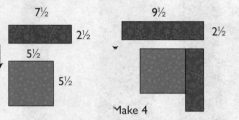

7½   9½

2½   2½

5½   5½   5½

Make 4

5. Sew one 2½" x 11½" Fabric D strip to one unit from step 4 as shown noting fabric extension. Press. Sew one 2½" x 13½" Fabric D strip to this unit as shown. Press. Make four.

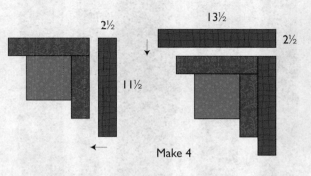

2½   13½

2½

11½

Make 4

6. Mark units from step 5 as shown (white dash line) and stay-stitch on drawn line. Sew one 1½" x 13½" Fabric C strip to one of these units. Press. Make two and label Unit 2, label remaining two units—Unit 1.

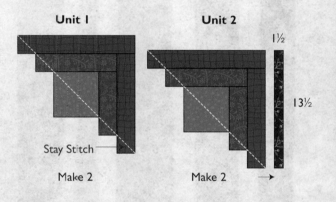

Unit 1   Unit 2

1½

13½

Stay Stitch

Make 2   Make 2

Leaves and berries link in 4-patch perfection on this earthy yet elegant table runner. The runner is deceptively simple to make with its diagonal construction.

7. Sew one Unit 1 from step 6 to one unit from step 2 as shown. Press. Make two.

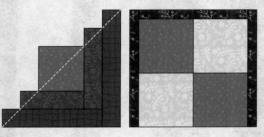

Make 2   ←

8. Sew unit from step 3 between two of Unit 2 from step 6 as shown, checking orientation of units prior to sewing. Press.

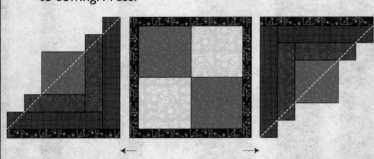

←   →

9. Referring to photo on page 13 and layout, sew unit from step 8 between two units from step 7. Press. Using a see-through ruler and rotary cutter, trim ends just past stay-stitching.

Adding the Appliqués

1. Refer to appliqué instructions on page 93. Our instructions are for Quick-Fuse Appliqué, but if you prefer hand appliqué add ¼"-wide seam allowance. Use Berry/Leaf Appliqué Pattern on page 17 to trace twelve sets of leaves on paper side of fusible web. Use leaf fabrics to prepare leaves for fusing.

2. Fuse fusible web to the wrong side of one 2" x 12" stem fabric piece. Cut fused fabric into three ¼" x 10¼" strips.

3. Referring to photo on page 13 and layout, arrange and fuse stems and leaves to table runner. Finish appliqué edges with machine satin stitch or other decorative stitching as desired. **Note:** We elected not to finish the edges of the appliqués; instead, during the quilting process, we stitched over all raw edges to hold them in place and to prevent raveling.

Layering and Finishing

1. Cut backing to measure 64" x 25". Referring to Layering the Quilt on page 94, arrange and baste backing, batting, and top together. Hand or machine quilt as desired.

2. Sew two 2¾" x 42" Fabric D strips end-to-end. Press. Make two. These will be used for the sides of table runner while Fabric C will be used for the pointed ends. Refer to Binding the Quilt on page 94 to prepare strips. Sew strips to sides first, then points, fold binding to the back in the same order and bind quilt to finish.

3. Referring to photo and layout, sew twelve ¾" buttons approximately ¾" away from each stem.

WILDBERRY
Table Runner
Finished Size: 59½" x 20¾"

WILDBERRY Placemat

Wildberry Placemat Finished Size: 16" x 20" For One Placemat	FIRST CUT		SECOND CUT	
	Number of Strips or Pieces	Dimensions	Number of Pieces	Dimensions
Fabric A Background ¼ yard	1	6½" x 42"	2	6½" squares
Fabric B Background and Light Triangles ¼ yard	1	6½" x 42"	2 8	6½" squares 4½" x 2½"
Fabric C Accent Border ⅛ yard	2	1" x 42"	2 2	1" x 13½" 1" x 12½"
Fabric D Border and Dark Triangles ¼ yard	1 2	2½" x 42" 2" x 42"	16 2 2	2½" squares 2" x 16½" 2" x 13½"
Backing - ½ yard		Lightweight Fusible Web - ¼ yard		
Batting - 18" x 22"		¾" Buttons - 4		
Leaf and Stem Appliqués - Assorted Scraps				

GETTING STARTED

Instructions are for one Wildberry Placemat. Adjust yardage and cuts for quantity desired. Read all instructions before beginning and use ¼"-wide seam allowance throughout. Read Cutting Strips and Pieces on page 92 prior to cutting fabric.

MAKING ONE PLACEMENT

1. Referring to layout, sew one 6½" Fabric B square to one 6½" Fabric A square. Press seam toward Fabric B. Make two. Sew these two units together, alternating colors. Press.

2. Referring to layout, sew unit from step 1 between two 1" x 12½" Fabric C strips. Press toward Fabric C. Sew this unit between two 1" x 13½" Fabric C strips. Press.

3. Referring to layout, sew unit from step 2 between two 2" x 13½" Fabric D strips. Press seams toward Fabric D. Sew this unit between two 2" x 16½" Fabric D strips. Press.

4. Refer to Quick Corner Triangles on page 92. Making quick corner triangle units, sew two 2½" Fabric D squares to one 4½" x 2½" Fabric B piece as shown. Press. Make eight.

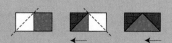

D = 2½ x 2½
B = 4½ x 2½
Make 8

5. Referring to layout, sew four units from step 4 together end-to-end. Press. Make two.

6. Referring to layout, sew unit from step 3 between two units from step 5. Press seams toward Fabric D.

ADDING THE APPLIQUÉS

Refer to appliqué instructions on page 93. Our instructions are for Quick-Fuse Appliqué, but if you prefer hand appliqué add ¼"-wide seam allowance.

1. Use Berry/Leaf Appliqué Pattern on page 17 to trace fours sets of leaves onto paper side of fusible web. Use leaf fabric to prepare appliqués for fusing.

2. Press fusible web to the wrong side of one 1" x 12" Stem fabric piece. Cut fused fabric into two ¼" x 10¼" strips.

3. Referring to layout and appliqué pattern on page 17, arrange and fuse stems and leaves to placemat. Finish appliqué edges with machine satin stitch or other decorative stitching if desired.

FINISHING THE PLACEMAT

1. Layer and center placemat top and backing right sides together on batting (wrong side of backing on batting.) Using ¼"-wide seam, stitch around placemat edges, leaving a 4" opening on one side for turning. Trim batting close to stitching and backing even with placemat edges. Clip corners, turn, and press. Hand-stitch opening closed.

2. Machine or hand quilt as desired. Referring to layout, sew buttons to placemat.

Debbie's
DECORATING TIPS

Decorating with fresh cut greenery is a centuries old tradition that is still the essence of Christmas today. The natural scents and rich colors and textures of fresh greenery evoke the warmth and tradition of the holidays. I love to cut greenery from my own backyard to fill my house with holiday spirit.

Bed Quilt
Make 3 and 3 Reversed

Wall Quilt
Make 1 and 1 Reversed

Moose Appliqué Pattern

Patterns are reversed for use
with Quick-Fuse Applique (page 93)

Tracing Line _____
Placement Line -·-·-·-·-·-·-
(will be hidden behind other fabrics)

Greenery and grapevines frame a garden sculpture to make a gorgeous wintertime wreath. Small cuttings, pinecones, and berries are wired together to ornament a grapevine wreath.

Fill a basket with fresh greenery, pinecones, and berries for a welcoming addition to the front porch or hearth. A mix of cuttings—long needle, short needle, cedar, and shrub—looks great in a natural color basket.

Berry/Leaf Appliqué Pattern

Stem Placement Guide ¼" × 13¾"

ACORN Ornaments

GETTING STARTED

Bring the outside in with these wooly woodland ornaments. 'Easy' is the word for these cute wool acorn ornaments, each embellished with assorted decorative machine stitches. To add fullness and texture to the wool, we felted it. See Tips for Felting Wool on page 95.

MAKING THE ORNAMENTS

1. These ornaments are a great place to try out your sewing machine's decorative stitches. Refer to sewing machine manual to select and stitch a variety of decorative stitches on wool piece.
   Optional: Hand embroider stitches on wool or stitch assorted beads to the top of each acorn after fusing.

2. Use patterns to trace acorns (top and bottom) in three different sizes on paper side of fusible web. Use appropriate wool or WoolFelt™ fabrics to prepare all appliqués for fusing. **Note:** Embroidered wool piece from step 1 is used for the tops of each acorn.

3. Using pattern paper or template plastic draw and cut out acorn background patterns. Using patterns, cut out one large, one medium, and one small acorn background from wool scrap.

4. Cut three 6" pieces of yarn for ornament hangers. Fold yarn in half and place on background piece placing cut ends toward center. Arrange and fuse acorn bottom then top pieces onto background piece, making sure the hanger ends are between layers and equal amounts of background wool show on all sides.

OPTIONAL METHOD

Refer to steps 1 and 2 to prepare appliqués. Instead of using background pattern piece, fuse acorn to a piece of background wool. Trim background piece approximately ⅛" away from fused acorn. Fold 6" piece of yarn in half and stitch to back of each ornament.

YOU WILL NEED...

- **YARN**
- **ASSORTED WOOL OR WOOLFELT™ SCRAPS**
- **HEAVYWEIGHT FUSIBLE WEB - ⅛ yard**

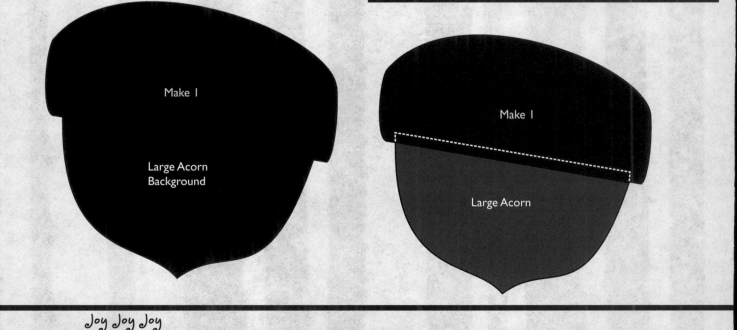

Make 1

Large Acorn Background

Make 1

Large Acorn

PRETTY AS A *Picture*

Frame a favorite ornament to add a festive touch to your holiday décor. Not only does it draw attention to a special ornament, it also adds dimension and interest to your wall. Just for fun, remove one picture in an arrangement and replace it with the framed ornament for a whimsical approach to holiday décor.

Sand frames lightly and remove residue. Paint larger frame Rich Espresso and small frame Festive Green. Two or more coats may be necessary for good coverage. Allow to dry. Using wood glue, center and glue small frame to large frame. Weigh down or clamp frames together and allow to dry. We chose to leave the back open so wall color shows through. If a back is desired, cut heavy cardboard to fit outside frame and paint or cover with scrapbook paper. Center ornament in the frame and use a thumbtack to hold in place.

YOU WILL NEED...

- **TWO UNPAINTED WOODEN FRAMES**
  That will stack together as shown. Outside measurements of ours are 8½" x 10½" and 6½" x 8½".
- **DECOART® DAZZLING METALLICS®**
  Festive Green and Rich Espresso
- **ASSORTED PAINTBRUSHES**
- **WOOD GLUE**
- **SANDPAPER**
- **ORNAMENT**

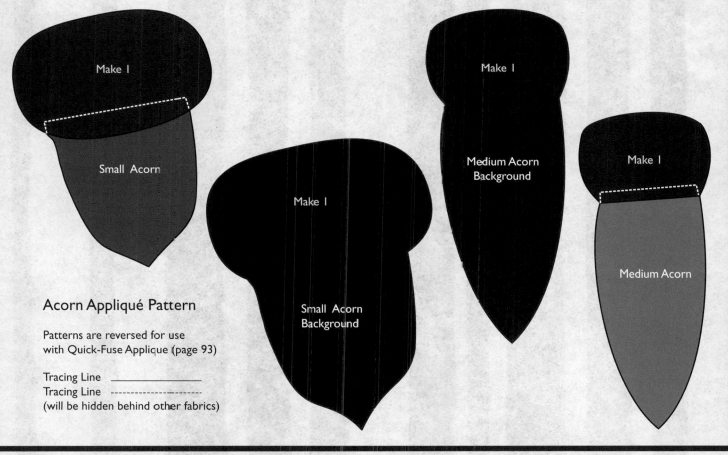

Make 1

Small Acorn

Make 1

Small Acorn Background

Make 1

Medium Acorn Background

Make 1

Medium Acorn

Acorn Appliqué Pattern

Patterns are reversed for use with Quick-Fuse Applique (page 93)

Tracing Line _____
Tracing Line ----------------------
(will be hidden behind other fabrics)

PINECONE
Pillow

GETTING STARTED

The play of textures—wools, cotton, yarn, and embroidery stitches—gives this pillow its rich allure. Read all instructions before beginning and use ¼"-wide seam allowance throughout.

MAKING THE PILLOW

Refer to appliqué instructions on page 93. Our instructions are for Quick-Fuse Appliqué.

1. Use patterns on page 21 to trace Pinecone and Pinecone Center, two regular and one reversed, on paper side of fusible web. Use appropriate wool scraps to prepare all appliqués for fusing.

2. Refer to Acorn Ornaments on page 18 steps 1-3, to prepare one Acorn and Acorn Background Pattern for embroidery stitching and fusing.

3. Press lightweight fusible web to one 4" x 10" wool piece for stems. Cut one 9" long strip ½"-wide at the base and tapering to ¼"-wide at the tip. Cut one 5" long strip ⅜"-wide at base and tapering to ¼"-wide at the tip. Cut two short ¼"-wide strips approximately 1" to 1½" in length.

YOU WILL NEED...

- **FABRIC A (Background)** - ⅜ yard (Wool)
  One 11½" x 18½" piece
- **FABRIC B (Border & Backing)** - ½ yard (Cotton)
  Two 11½" x 18½" pieces (Backing)
  Two 3" x 18½" pieces (Border)
- **APPLIQUÉS** - Assorted wool scraps
  One 4" x 10" (Stem)
- **FABRIC STABILIZER** - ½ yard
- **BROWN YARN**
- **VARIEGATED GREEN YARN**
- **LIGHTWEIGHT FUSIBLE WEB** - ⅓ yard
- **16" x 18" PILLOW FORM or**
  OPTIONAL PILLOW FORM - ½ yard
  Two 16½" x 18½" pieces
  Fiberfill

Finished Size: 18" x 16"

Rustic wool creates picturesque pinecones on this warm and welcoming pillow. Embroidered accents create the illusion of pine needles.

4. Refer to photo to position and fuse appliqués to 11½" x 18½" Fabric A wool piece.

5. Place a piece of fabric stabilizer or interfacing behind unit from step 4 to give it extra strength. Sew this unit between two 3" x 18½" Fabric B strips. Press seams toward Fabric B.

6. Refer to photo above and Embroidery Stitch Guide on page 95. Using a strand of brown yarn, stitch single Fly Stitches scattering stitches randomly on pinecone center pieces, going through all layers.

7. Referring to photo and using a variegated yarn, stitch long single stitches for each pine needle as desired. Referring to Big Stitch Quilting on page 10 and using brown yarn, stitch a straight line ⅜" from seam line.

8. Refer to Finishing Pillows, page 95, steps 2-4 and use two 11" x 18½" backing pieces to sew backing.

9. Insert 16" x 18" pillow form or refer to Pillow Forms on page 95 and use two 16½" x 18½" pieces of fabric and fiberfill to make a pillow form if desired.

Pinecone Pillow Appliqués

Patterns are reversed for use
with Quick-Fuse Applique (page 93)

Tracing Line _____
Tracing Line ----------------------
(will be hidden behind other fabrics)

Pinecone Pillow
Acorn Background
Make 1

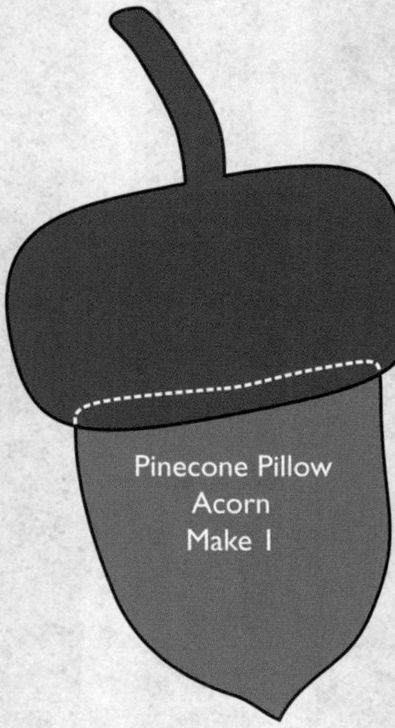

Pinecone Pillow
Acorn
Make 1

Pinecone
Make 2 and
1 Reversed

Pinecone Center
Make 2 and
1 Reversed

Organic Glitz Tree

Set the tone for an elegant yet woodsy holiday with this gilt tree. Experiment with various techniques, try out different glitters, and glue on lots of beads for an intriguing decoration that you'll love using year after year. There's no right or wrong with this project—the more glitz you add the better the tree looks, so have some fun!

You Will Need...

- **15" Styrofoam® Cone**
- **Metallic Wrapping Paper and/or tissue**
- **Mod Podge® Gloss**
- **Various Paintbrushes**
- **Metal Leaf Adhesive**
- **Gold Metal Leaf**
- **Various Gold and Copper Glitters***
- **Glittery Leaves and Disks****
- **Various Seed, Tube, and Small Beads**
- **Craft Tacky Glue (Must Dry Clear)**
- **Small Bird Ornament For Top (Optional)**
- **Terracotta Flowerpot and Saucer**
- **Delta Ceramcoat® Acrylic paint
  - Burnt Umber**

*We especially like Ultra Fine Glitter.
**We cut apart purchased holiday sprays for glittery leaves and disks.
Note: Hot glue can melt Styrofoam, so use only low temperature hot glue if desired.

Making the Tree

Refer to photo as needed.
1. Tear wrapping and tissue paper into small (2") irregularly shaped pieces.

2. Using paintbrush, spread Mod Podge® on a portion of the cone and cover with torn paper squares. Cover with more Mod Podge® and smooth down with paintbrush. Continue process, overlapping edges of papers, until entire cone is covered. It will look milky, but dries clear. Allow to dry.

3. Use tacky glue to adhere glittery leaves and disks to cone. If needed, use straight pins to hold large items flat and in place until dry.

4. Following manufacturer's directions, apply metal leaf adhesive in irregular shapes and random places on the cone. When 'set' according to the manufacturer's directions, apply gold leaf to all adhesive spots. Brush away excess gold leaf with a dry paintbrush.

5. Spread tacky glue onto cone in irregular shapes and random places. Sprinkle with various colors and types of glitter and/or beads as desired. Let dry.

6. When thoroughly dry, use same techniques to add more color, sparkle, or bead texture wherever needed. Glue bird or ornament to top of tree.

7. Following manufacturer's directions, apply metal leaf adhesive to flowerpot and saucer. When 'set' apply gold leaf and brush away excess with paintbrush. Dip paintbrush into Burnt Umber paint, blot on paper towel and dry brush Burnt Umber accents onto flowerpot and saucer.

BERRY MERRY CHRISTMAS
Stockings

GETTING STARTED

These rich wool stockings add a touch of warmth to any Christmas setting. Read all instructions before beginning. We felted the wool prior to cutting to add texture and weight. Please see Tips for Felting Wool on page 95 before purchasing wool. Wool will shrink when felted so yardage may need to be adjusted.

MAKING THE STOCKING

1. Refer to Berry Merry Stocking Pattern and instructions on pages 24-25. Trace all sections aligning placement lines to make a complete stocking pattern.

2. Using stocking pattern, trace and cut from wool fabric one stocking (front) and one reversed (back).

3. Refer to appliqué instructions on page 93 and Leaf Appliqué Pattern on page 25. Refer to photo as a guide for the number of leaves and stems needed for each stocking arrangement. Trace desired number of leaves and stem for project on paper side of fusible web. Use appropriate fabrics to prepare all appliqués for fusing. **Note:** We elected to free hand a longer s-curved stem for one stocking.

4. Referring to photo, position and fuse appliqués to stocking front. Stitch down the center of each piece to hold in place, wool does not ravel eliminating the need for finishing edges.

YOU WILL NEED...
For One Stocking

- **STOCKING** - ½ yard Red Wool
  One ½" x 6" Piece for loop
- **CUFF** - ⅓ yard Ivory Wool
  One 8½" x 16" Piece
- **LEAF & STEM APPLIQUÉS** - Scraps
- **LIGHTWEIGHT FUSIBLE WEB** - ⅓ yard
- **1¾" FRINGE** - ⅝ yard
- **⅝" BUTTONS** - 5
- **ASSORTED RED & YELLOW BEADS** - 20 to 30
- **EMBROIDERY FLOSS**

Your Christmas will be berry merry when Santa fills these stockings! Buttons, beads, and fringe embellish these striking stockings.

5. Referring to photo, arrange and sew beads to stocking front.

6. Place stocking pieces wrong sides together, matching all edges. Refer to Embroidery Stitch Guide and using four strands of floss and a blanket stitch, stitch around edges leaving top free of stitches.

7. With right sides together, sew 8½" ends of cuff piece together. Press seam open. Fold cuff in half lengthwise, wrong sides together.

8. Fold ½" x 6" wool piece in half, place loop inside stocking at seam allowance (heel side), matching ends with stocking edge. Baste ⅛" from outside edge. Place folded cuff inside stocking, aligning raw edges and stitch cuff to stocking. Turn cuff to right side of stocking and pull loop out.

9. Referring to photo hand stitch fringe to bottom edge of cuff. Arrange and sew five buttons to cuff as desired.

MAKING THE BERRY MERRY CHRISTMAS STOCKING PATTERN

Trace and cut out Stocking Pattern, Parts 1 and 2. Tape together matching markings. Extend top of Stocking Pattern by attaching an 8½" x 11" paper at star markings. Align straight edges and mark paper as shown.

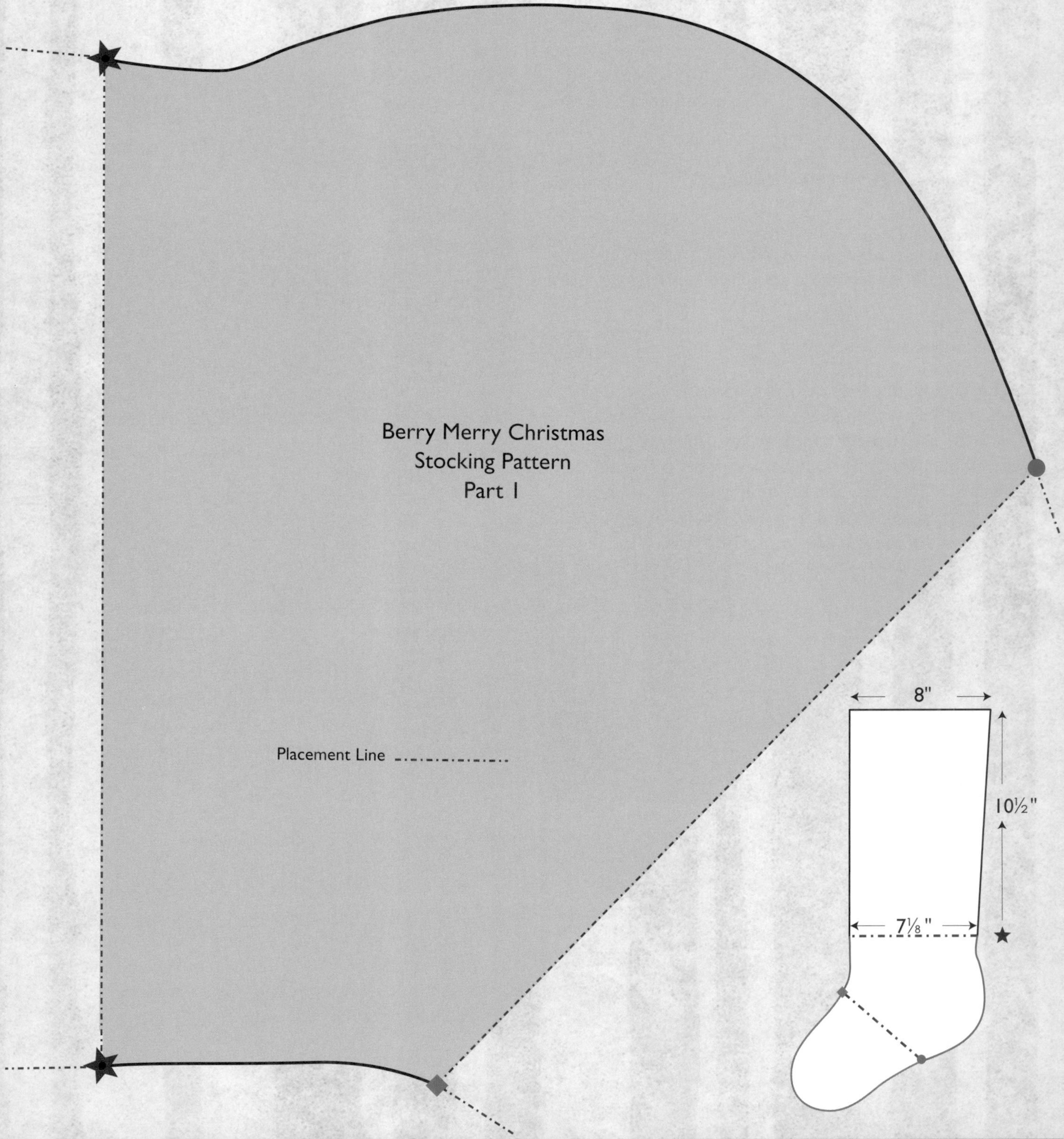

Berry Merry Christmas
Stocking Pattern
Part 1

Placement Line ·–··–··–·

8"

10½"

7⅛"

Berry Merry
Christmas Stocking
Leaf Appliqués
Pattern

Berry Merry Christmas
Stocking Pattern
Part 2

Placement Line _.._.._.._.._.._.

Jingle Joys

A Chic and Playful approach to the Holidays. Bold Colors and whimsical motifs make this holiday collection a fun loving family favorite.

Ornaments and fanciful trees are featured in a wall quilt, tree skirt, and pillows. Bells and an abundance of trims highlight stockings, table runner, ornaments, and much more.

ORNAMENT
Wall Quilt

FABRIC REQUIREMENTS AND CUTTING INSTRUCTIONS

Read all instructions before beginning and use ¼"-wide seam allowance throughout. Read Cutting Strips and Pieces on page 92 prior to cutting fabric.

GETTING STARTED

This quilt will bring back fond memories of past Christmas trees and searching through the boughs to locate favorite ornaments. Three different 8" square blocks (unfinished), each decked out with a unique style, are accented with assorted trims and embellishments. Refer to Accurate Seam Allowance on page 92. Whenever possible use the Assembly Line Method on page 92. Press seams in the direction of arrows.

MAKING THE BACKGROUND BLOCKS

Reminder: When joining bias and straight edge fabrics, place bias edge against the feed dogs to help prevent stretching of unit.

1. Sew three different 3" x 26" Fabric A strips together lengthwise to make a strip set. Make six, each using a different fabric combination. Press to one side. Cut strip sets into forty-eight 3"-wide segments.

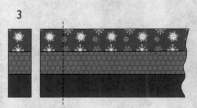

3

Make 6 strip sets
(each using a different combination)
Cut 48 segments

Ornament Wall Quilt Finished Size: 53" Square	FIRST CUT		SECOND CUT	
	Number of Strips or Pieces	Dimensions	Number of Pieces	Dimensions
Fabric A ⅓ yard each of 9 fabrics Nine-Patch Background *Cut from each fabric	1* 2*	3⅜" x 42" 3" x 42"	3* 1* 2* 5*	3⅜" squares 2⅝" x 4" 3" x 26" 3" squares
Fabric B ⅓ yard Ornament	1	8" x 42"	3	8" squares
Fabric C ⅓ yard Ornament	2	4¾" x 42"		
Fabric D ⅜ yard Ornament	2	5¾" x 42"		
Fabric E ⅛ yard Ornament Top	1	3" x 42"	9	3" squares
Fabric F ½ yard Block Accent	1 1	12" x 42" 4" x 42"	3 4	12" squares (Cut twice diagonally) 4" squares
Fabric G ⅛ yard Ornament Accent	1	2" x 42"		
Fabric H ⅛ yard Ornament Accent	2	1¼" x 42"		
Fabric I ⅛ yard Ornament Accent	1	1¾" x 42"		
BORDERS				
First Border ¼ yard	5	1¼" x 42"		
Second Border ¼ yard	5	1" x 42"		
Outside Border & Binding 1⅛ yards	5 6	4" x 43" 2¾" x 42"		

Backing - 3⅓ yards
Batting - 59" x 59"
Holly Appliqués - Felt or felted wool scraps

Assorted Trims
Assorted Buttons and Bells

2. Arrange and sew three assorted segments from step 1 together as shown. Press. Make sixteen and label Block 1. Block measures 8" square.

Block 1

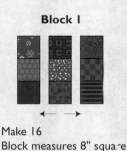

Make 16
Block measures 8" square

3. Refer to Making Quick Corner Triangles on page 92. Making quick corner triangle units, sew two 3⅜" Fabric A squares to one Fabric F triangle as shown. Align marked square corner to triangle tip as shown and pin in place. Sew on marked line. Cut ¼" away from stitches and trim fabric overhang as shown even with triangle piece. Press. Make twelve.

A = 3⅜ x 3⅜
F = Triangle
Make 12

4. Making a quick corner triangle unit, sew one 3" Fabric A square to unit from step 3 as shown. Press. Make twelve and label Side Setting Triangles.

Side Setting Triangles

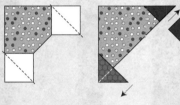

A = 3 x 3
Unit from step 3
Make 12

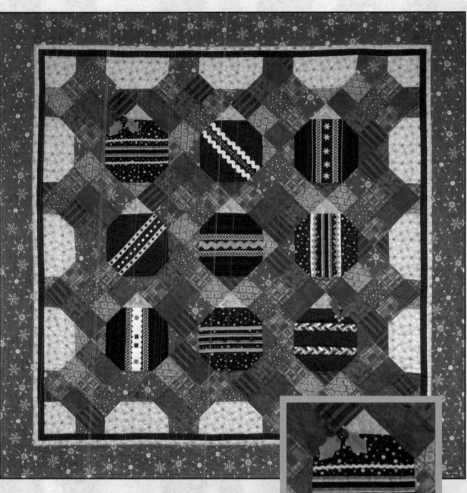

Colorful ornaments hide among the boughs of green fabric on this eye-catching quilt. Strip-piecing and attaching trims before the ornament blocks are sewn in make this project fast and fun.

5. Sew one 4" Fabric F square to one 2⅝" x 4" Fabric A piece as shown. Press. Sew this unit to one 2⅝" x 4" Fabric A piece. Press. Cut diagonally as shown. Make four and label Corner Triangles.

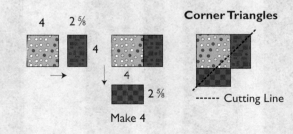

4   2⅝

4

4

2⅝

Corner Triangles

------ Cutting Line

Make 4

MAKING THE ORNAMENT BLOCKS

These blocks are set on point with gold triangle at the top of each ornament. Check placement of center strip prior to sewing Fabric E squares to obtain the desired effect. Trims are sewn to center units prior to making quick corner triangles to complete blocks. Buttons, holly leaves, and jingle bells are added after quilting.

1. Sew one 2" x 42" Fabric G strip between two 5¾" x 42" Fabric D strips as shown. Press.

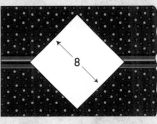

2. Using a see-through ruler and rotary cutter, cut three 8" squares from strip-pieced unit making sure center strip is centered and on point in square as shown.

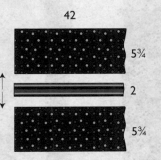

Cut 3

3. Referring to photo on page 29 and layout, arrange and sew trim to unit from step 2 as desired.

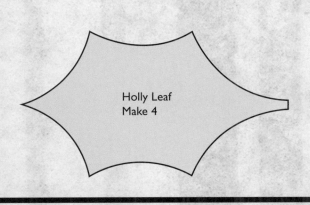

Holly Leaf
Make 4

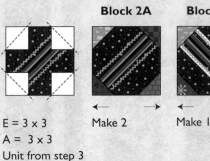

ORNAMENT Wall Quilt
Finished Size: 53" Square

4. Refer to Quick Corner Triangles on page 92. Making quick corner triangle units, sew one 3" Fabric E square and three 3" Fabric A squares to unit from step 3 as shown. Press. Make three and label two Block 2A and one Block 2B. Note placement of Fabric E prior to sewing. Block measures 8" square.

Block 2A   **Block 2B**

Make 2   Make 1

E = 3 x 3
A = 3 x 3
Unit from step 3
Block measures 8" square

5. Referring to photo on page 29 and layout, arrange and sew trim to three 8" Fabric B squares as desired.

6. Making quick corner triangle units, sew one 3" Fabric E square and three 3" Fabric A squares to unit from step 5 as shown. Press. Make three and label Block 3. Block measures 8" square.

Block 3

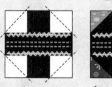

E = 3 x 3
A = 3 x 3
Unit from step 5
Make 3
Block measures 8" square

7. Arrange and sew two 4¾" x 42" Fabric C strips, two 1¼" x 42" Fabric H strips, and one 1¾" x 42" Fabric I strip together as shown. Press. Referring to diagram below cut three 8" squares, placing center strip, on point as shown.

42

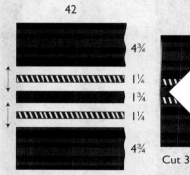

4¾
1¼
1¾
1¼
4¾

8

Cut 3

8. Referring to photo on page 29 and layout, arrange and sew trims to unit from step 7 as desired.

9. Making quick corner triangle units, sew one 3" Fabric E square and three 3" Fabric A squares to unit from step 8 as shown. Press. Make three and label two Block 4A and one Block 4B. Note placement of Fabric E prior to sewing. Block measures 8" square.

Block 4A   **Block 4B**

E = 3 x 3
A = 3 x 3   Make 2   Make 1
Unit from step 8
Block measures 8" square

Referring to photo on page 29

Debbie's
DECORATING TIPS

Fun with Ornaments!
Ornaments can do a lot more than hang on a tree! Some ornaments are so special that they deserve a place of honor in your decorating scheme.

Special ornaments receive top billing when placed in a shallow glass bowl. A supporting cast of plain ornaments balances out the arrangement. A sprig of berries, beaded candy canes and a glass snowflake provide a backdrop for our special Santa and striped ornament. A layer of faux snow helps hold ornaments in place.

These polka dot ornaments are so much fun that we placed them on pedestals! Glass candlesticks are just right to hold the ornaments high, especially when they are accented with beaded napkin holders pressed into service as mini-wreaths. Ornaments are turned upside down and a little Blu Tack® helps hold everything in place.

ASSEMBLY

Referring to photo on page 29 and step diagrams in this section, **arrange all blocks prior to sewing top.**
Note: Orientation of Side Setting Triangles changes for Rows 5 & 6.

1. Sew one Corner Triangle to one Block 1. Press. Sew this unit between two Side Setting Triangles as shown. Press. Make two. Label Rows 1 and 7.

2. Arrange and sew together two Side Setting Triangles, two of Block 1, and one Block 4A as shown. Press. Make two. **Note:** Change orientation of Side Setting Triangles for Row 6. Label Rows 2 and 6.

3. Arrange and sew together two Side Setting Triangles, three of Block 1, one Block 3, and one Block 2B as shown. Press. Make two. **Note:** Sew Blocks 1, 3, 2A and change orientation of Side Setting Triangles for Row 5. Label Rows 3 and 5.

4. Arrange and sew together two Corner Triangles, four of Block 1, one Block 2A, one Block 4B, and one Block 3 as shown. Press and label Row 4.

5. Referring to photo on page 29 and layout on page 30, arrange and sew together Rows 1-7. Press.

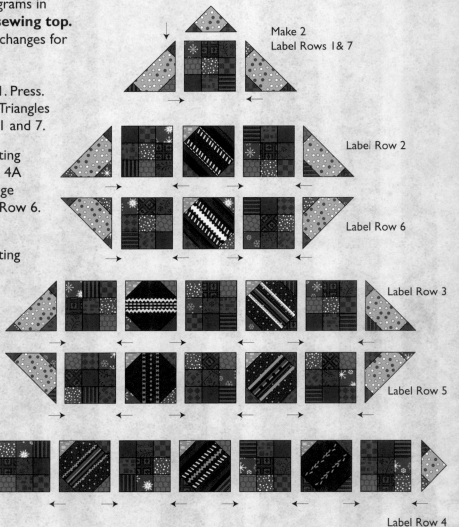

Make 2
Label Rows 1 & 7

Label Row 2

Label Row 6

Label Row 3

Label Row 5

Label Row 4

FINISHING THE QUILT

1. Sew 1¼" x 42" First Border strips together end-to-end to make one continuous 1¼"-wide First Border strip. Referring to Adding the Borders on page 94, measure quilt through center from side to side. Cut two 1¼"-wide First Border strips to this measurement. Sew to top and bottom of quilt. Press seams toward border.

2. Measure quilt through center from top to bottom including border just added. Cut two 1¼"-wide First Border strips to this measurement. Sew to sides of quilt. Press.

3. Refer to steps 1 and 2 to join, measure, trim, and sew 1"-wide Second Border and 4"-wide Outside Border strips to top, bottom, and sides of quilt. Press.

4. Cut backing crosswise into two equal pieces. Sew pieces together lengthwise to make one 60" x 80" (approximate) backing piece. Press and trim to 60" x 60".

5. Referring to Layering the Quilt on page 94, arrange and baste backing, batting, and top together. Hand or machine quilt as desired.

6. Refer to Binding the Quilt on page 94. Sew 2¾" x 42" binding strips end-to-end to make one continuous 2¾"-wide binding strip. Bind quilt to finish.

7. Refer to Holly Leaf Pattern on page 30 to trace and cut four leaves from felted wool scraps. Felt does not ravel so there's no need to finish edges. Using embroidery floss, hand-stitch leaves to wall quilt by stitching a center vein on each leaf. Attach buttons, beads or bells to ornament blocks as desired.

ORNAMENT Banner

Quick GIFT IDEA!

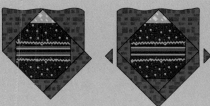

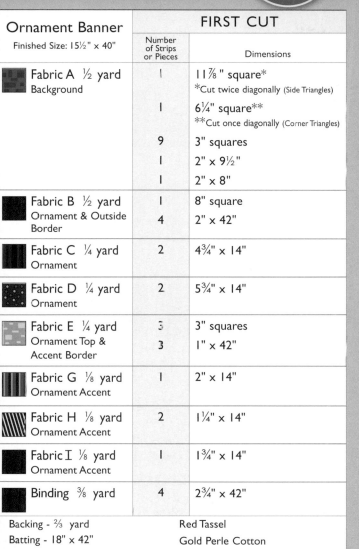

Ornament Banner Finished Size: 15½" x 40"	FIRST CUT	
	Number of Strips or Pieces	Dimensions
Fabric A ½ yard Background	1	11⅞" square* *Cut twice diagonally (Side Triangles)
	1	6¼" square** **Cut once diagonally (Corner Triangles)
	9	3" squares
	1	2" x 9½"
	1	2" x 8"
Fabric B ½ yard Ornament & Outside Border	1	8" square
	4	2" x 42"
Fabric C ¼ yard Ornament	2	4¾" x 14"
Fabric D ¼ yard Ornament	2	5¾" x 14"
Fabric E ¼ yard Ornament Top & Accent Border	3	3" squares
	3	1" x 42"
Fabric G ⅛ yard Ornament Accent	1	2" x 14"
Fabric H ⅛ yard Ornament Accent	2	1¼" x 14"
Fabric I ⅛ yard Ornament Accent	1	1¾" x 14"
Binding ⅜ yard	4	2¾" x 42"
Backing - ⅔ yard Batting - 18" x 42"	Red Tassel Gold Perle Cotton	

Making the Banner

1. Refer to Ornament Wall Quilt on pages 30-31, Making the Ornament Blocks, steps 1-9, to make three ornament blocks, one each of Block 2A, 3, and 4A. Strips sets are constructed using 14" lengths of Fabric C, D, G, H, and I strips instead of 42" lengths.

2. Referring to layout, arrange blocks from step 1 and Fabric A triangle pieces, for diagonal row construction. Sew Block 3 between one Fabric A side and one Fabric A Corner Triangle piece. Press toward Fabric A. Sew remaining Fabric A Corner Triangle piece to this unit. Press.

3. Sew Block 4A between two Fabric A Side Triangle pieces. Press seams toward Fabric A.

4. Sew one Fabric A Side Triangle piece to Block 2A. Press seam toward Fabric A.

5. Referring to layout, arrange and sew together units from steps 2-4. Press.

6. Sew 2" x 8" Fabric A piece to unit from step 5. Press toward Fabric A. Sew this unit to one 2" x 9½" Fabric A piece to adjoining corner. Press and trim as shown.

7. Referring to Adding the Borders on page 94, measure quilt through center from side to side. Cut one 1"-wide Fabric E strip to this measurement. Sew to top of banner. Press seams toward border.

8. Measure quilt along side edges including border just added. Cut two 1"-wide Fabric E strips to this measurement. Sew to sides of quilt. Press and trim border to match angle. Measure bottom angle edges, cut one 1"-wide strip to this measurement and sew to bottom of quilt. Repeat to add other bottom border. Press and trim to match sides.

9. Referring to steps 7 and 8 measure, trim, and sew 2"-wide Outside Border strips to top, sides and bottom of quilt. Press.

Finishing the Quilt

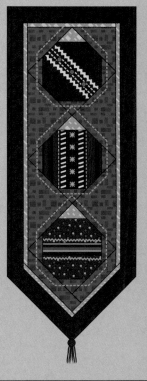

1. Referring to Layering the Quilt on page 94, arrange and baste backing, batting, and top together. Hand or machine quilt as desired. Refer to Big Stitch Quilting Technique on page 10. Using gold Perle Cotton, stitch around ornaments as indicated in layout.

2. Sew 2¾" x 42" binding strips end-to-end to make one continuous 2¾"-wide binding strip. Refer to Binding the Quilt on page 94 and bind quilt to finish, adding side bindings last.

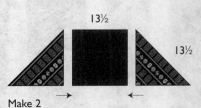

JOYFUL
Tree Skirt

MAKING THE TREE SKIRT

1. Sew one 13½" Fabric A square between two Fabric B triangles as shown. Press. Make two.

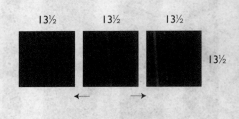

13½

13½

Make 2 →   ←

Joyful Tree Skirt Finished Size: 39" x 39"	FIRST CUT		SECOND CUT	
	Number of Strips or Pieces	Dimensions	Number of Pieces	Dimensions
Fabric A Background ⅞ yard	2	13½" x 42"	5	13½" squares
Fabric B Triangles ⅝ yard	4	"Fussy Cut" Triangles		
Fabric C Trees ⅝ yard	2	10½" x 42"	4	10½" x 13½"

Backing - 1¼ yards (must measure at least 42" wide)
Batting - 42" x 42"
Tree Trunk Appliqués - scraps
Lightweight Fusible Web - 1½ yards
Pompom Trim - 4 yards
3"-wide Fringe - 4 yards
Pattern Paper or Template Plastic

FABRIC REQUIREMENTS AND CUTTING INSTRUCTIONS

Read all instructions before beginning and use ¼"-wide seam allowance throughout. Read Cutting Strips and Pieces on page 92 prior to cutting fabric.

GETTING STARTED

Christmas just wouldn't be Christmas without a tree! Make this fast-to-construct, striking, designer tree skirt to adorn your tree. Refer to Accurate Seam Allowance on page 92. Press seams in the direction of arrows.

MAKING TRIANGLE PATTERN

1. Draw a 13½" square on template plastic or pattern paper, cut once diagonally to make a triangle pattern.

2. Using pattern from step 1 cut four triangles from Fabric B piece. If using directional fabric place stripe or motif to be featured ¼" away from pattern along outside edge to allow for seam allowances. Mark registration lines on pattern to aid in cutting matching triangle pieces. Cut four Fabric B triangles.

2. Sew three 13½" Fabric A squares together as shown. Press.

13½   13½   13½

13½

←   →

3. Sew unit from step 2 between two units from step 1. Press.

ADDING THE APPLIQUÉS

Refer to appliqué instructions on page 93. Our instructions are for Quick-Fuse Appliqué, but if you prefer hand appliqué add ¼"-wide seam allowance.

1. Cut four 10" x 13" lightweight fusible web pieces. Mark center on one 13" side as shown. Draw a line from corner to center then back to opposite corner as shown to make a triangular tree shape. Cut ½" beyond drawn lines.

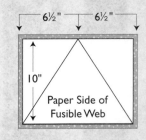

6½"   6½"

10"

Paper Side of Fusible Web

2. Following manufacturer's instructions, press fusible web to the wrong side of 10½" x 13½" Fabric C piece. Cut on drawn line and bottom edge to make tree appliqué. Make four.

3. Use Tree Trunk pattern to trace trunk on paper side of fusible web. Use fabric scraps to prepare appliqués for fusing.

4. Referring to layout on page 36, fuse tree and trunk appliqués to tree skirt. Finish appliqué edges with machine satin stitch or other decorative stitching as desired.

FINISHING THE TREE SKIRT

1. On wrong side of tree skirt, mark a 4" circle in center square and draw a diagonal line from circle to outside edge through one side triangle as shown.

Tree Trunk
Make 4

Joyful Tree Skirt
Appliqué Pattern

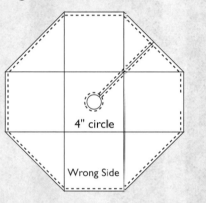

4" circle

Wrong Side

2. Layer and center marked skirt top and backing right sides together on batting, wrong side of backing on batting. Using ¼"-wide seam as shown in diagram above, stitch around center circle, on each side of drawn diagonal line and around outside edge. Leave a 6-8" opening on a straight edge for turning.

Trees and trims dance around the Christmas tree on this unique octagonal tree skirt. Use a fun repeating stripe for even more pizzazz.

Debbie's DECORATING TIPS

Jingle All the Way!
Decorate your home with the joyful jingle of bells. Jingle bells are available in many sizes and colors and make charming and playful accents in any setting. I love combining bells and Christmas candies for a playful approach to the holidays.

3. Cut on drawn lines. Trim batting close to stitching and backing even with outside edge of the tree skirt. Clip corners, turn, and press. Hand-stitch opening closed.

4. Quilt as desired. Sew fringe and pompoms to outside edge of tree skirt, turning under at opening. Referring to photo on page 35 and layout, embellish as desired. We elected to use large hole sequins and paillettes from a garland that we took apart. Buttons, small sequins, and other trims will also work well. If you plan to launder the tree skirt, select suitable embellishments.

JOYFUL
Tree Skirt

This cute centerpiece started with a glass cylinder vase. Large peppermint candy sticks circle the cylinder and are held in place by rubber bands covered with pretty ribbons. The vase was filled with fresh greenery and accented by small jingle bells mounted on florist wire. The candy-covered vase was placed on a metallic green plate and large red bells and chocolate kisses finish this delectable centerpiece.

For another table centerpiece, we combined a variety of jingle bells and small ornaments in a simple wooden bowl. Apple green is a trendy color for Christmas and gives our centerpiece a fresh new look. Everything in the bowl is red or apple green, but the variety of sizes and finishes makes each item stand out.

BEADED Garland Tree

Create an eye-catching centerpiece in minutes with bead garland and a tree-shaped cone.

Use low temperature hot glue to adhere the first couple of rows of garland to the tree, then simply wrap the garland around the cone. Use straight pins to hold garland in place every two or three rows or as needed. Use low temperature hot glue to secure the last row to the cone. Glue an ornament or bell to the top of the tree.

YOU WILL NEED...

- **GREEN STYROFOAM® CONE**
  (Ours is 15")
- **BEAD GARLAND**
  (Amount will vary with the size of beads. Our beads are about $5/16$" round and it took three 9' garlands to cover the tree.)
- **GLUE GUN & LOW TEMPERATURE GLUE STICKS**
- **STRAIGHT PINS**
- **ORNAMENT OR BELL FOR TREE TOP**

JINGLE JOYS Stockings

JINGLE BELLS STOCKING

GETTING STARTED

These Christmas stockings are quick to make and add a whimsical touch to the holiday season. Read all instructions before beginning and use ¼"-wide seam allowance throughout.

MAKING THE STOCKING

1. Refer to Jingle Joys Stocking pattern and instructions on pages 42-43. Trace all sections aligning placement lines to make a complete stocking pattern.

2. Place stocking fabric right side up on batting. Quilt as desired. Using stocking pattern, cut one front and one back (reversed) from quilted fabric.

3. Using stocking pattern, cut one front and one back (reversed) from lining fabric.

4. Place stocking pieces right sides together, matching all edges. Using ¼"-wide seam, sew around edges leaving top edge free of stitching. Turn stocking right side out and press.

5. Place lining pieces right sides together, matching all edges. Using ¼"-wide seam, sew around edges leaving top edge free of stitching.

6. Place lining inside stocking, wrong sides together, and edge-stitch in place.

7. Fold ½" x 6" felt loop piece in half, place loop inside stocking at seam allowance (heel side), matching ends with stocking edge. Stay-stitch ⅛" from outside edge.

8. With right sides together, sew 8½" ends of 8½" x 16" cuff piece together. Press seam open. Fold cuff in half lengthwise with wrong sides together.

9. Place folded cuff inside stocking, aligning raw edges and stitch cuff to stocking. Turn cuff to right side of stocking and pull loop out.

10. Referring to photo sew decorative trims and small jingle bells to cuff.

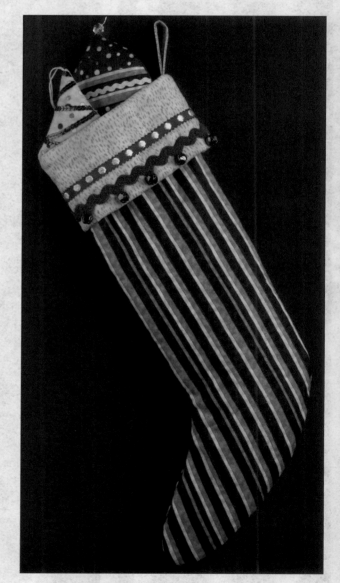

Santa won't miss these stockings! Colorful and cute, these stockings are also quick-to-make.

YOU WILL NEED...

- **STOCKING** - ½ yard
- **LINING** - ½ yard
- **CUFF** - ⅓ yard
  One 8½" x 16" piece
- **LOOP** - One ½" x 6" piece (Felt)
- **BATTING** - 18" x 40"
- **WIDE RICKRACK TRIM** - ½ yard
- **TRIM** - ½ yard
- **SMALL JINGLE BELLS** - 5

Radiant Stars Stocking

Getting Started

Stars glow on this stocking and can be any color to fit your home decorating needs. Make several for yourself, or make one as a gift for a friend and fill with Christmas goodies. Read all instructions before beginning and use ¼"-wide seam allowance throughout.

Making the Stocking

1. Refer to Color and Joy Stocking pattern on pages 42-43. Trace all sections aligning placement lines to make a complete stocking pattern.

2. Place stocking fabric right side up on batting. Quilt as desired. Using stocking pattern, cut one front and one back (reversed) from quilted fabric.

3. Using stocking pattern, cut one front and one back (reversed) from lining fabric.

4. Refer to appliqué instructions on page 93 and Star Appliqué Pattern below. Trace five stars on paper side of fusible web. Use fabric scraps to prepare star appliqués for fusing.

5. Referring to photo, position and fuse appliqués to stocking front. Finish appliqué edges with machine satin stitch or other decorative stitching as desired.

6. Place stocking pieces right side together, matching all edges. Using ¼"-wide seam, sew around edges leaving top edge free of stitching. Turn stocking right side out and press.

7. Place lining pieces right side together, matching all edges. Using ¼"-wide seam, sew around edges leaving top edge free of stitching.

8. Place lining inside stocking, wrong sides together, and edge-stitch in place.

9. Fold ½" x 6" loop piece in half, place loop inside stocking at seam allowance (heel side), matching ends with stocking edge. Stay stitch ⅛" from outside edge.

10. With right sides together, sew 8½" ends of 8½" x 16" lengthwise cuff piece together. Press seam open. Fold cuff in half with wrong sides together.

11. Place folded cuff inside stocking, aligning raw edges and stitch cuff to stocking. Turn cuff to right side of stocking and pull loop out. Attach jingle bells to loop.

Star Appliqué Pattern

You Will Need...

- **Stocking** - ½ yard
- **Lining** - ½ yard
- **Cuff** - ⅓ yard
  One 8½" x 16" piece
- **Loop** - One ½" x 6" piece (Felt)
- **Batting** - 18" x 40"
- **Star Appliqués** - Scraps
- **Lightweight Fusible Web** - ⅛ yard
- **Two Large Jingle Bells & Cording**

MAKING THE JINGLE JOYS STOCKING PATTERN

Trace and cut out Stocking Pattern, Parts 1 and 2. Tape together matching markings. Extend top of Stocking Pattern by attaching an 8½" x 11" paper at star markings. Align straight edges and mark paper as shown.

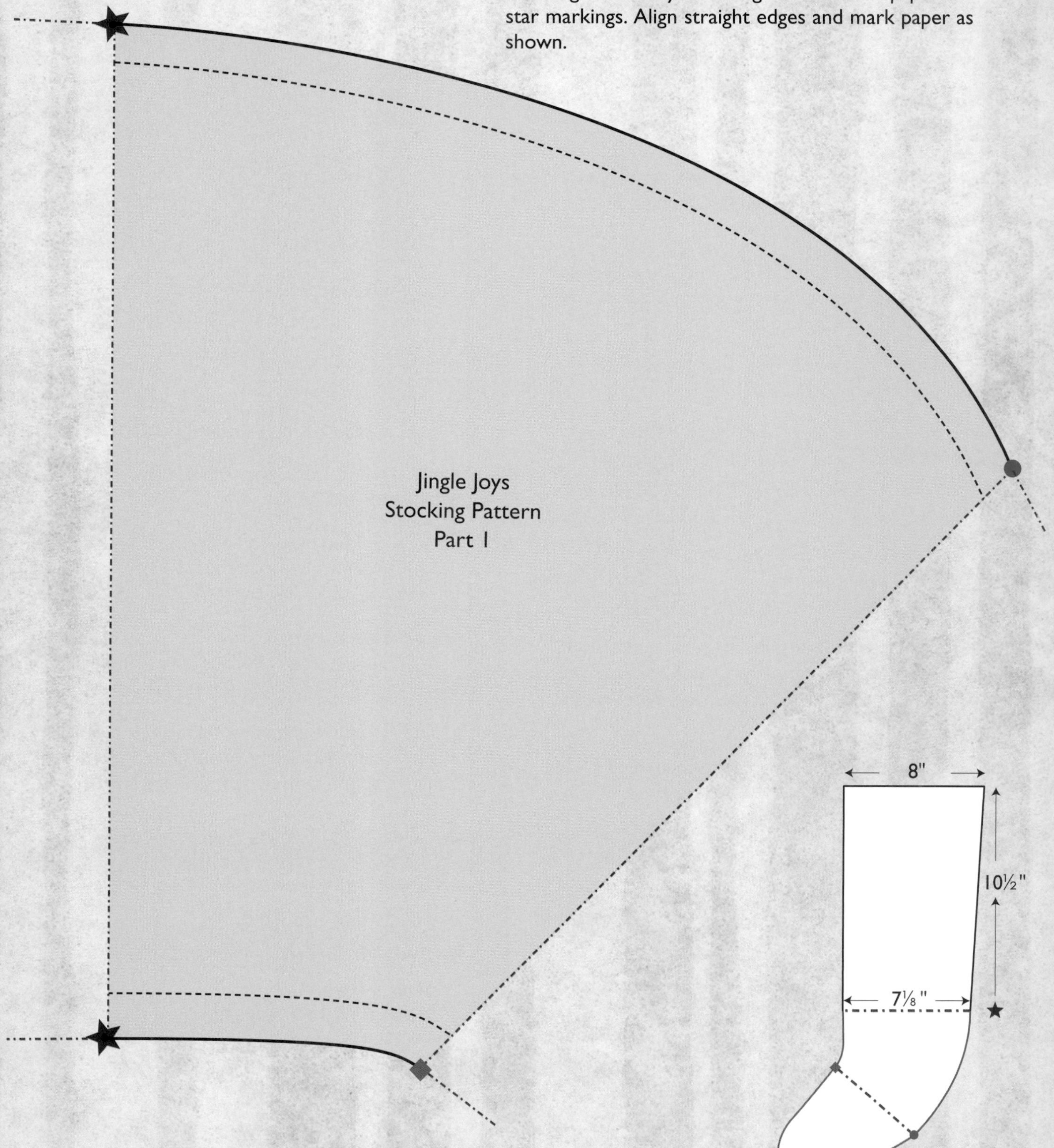

Jingle Joys
Stocking Pattern
Part 1

8"

10½"

7⅛"

Joy Joy Joy

Stitch Lines -------------

Placement Line --·--·--·--

Y o T

Christmas Joys Pillow
JOY Appliqué Pattern

Pattern is reversed for use
with Quick-Fuse Applique (page 93)

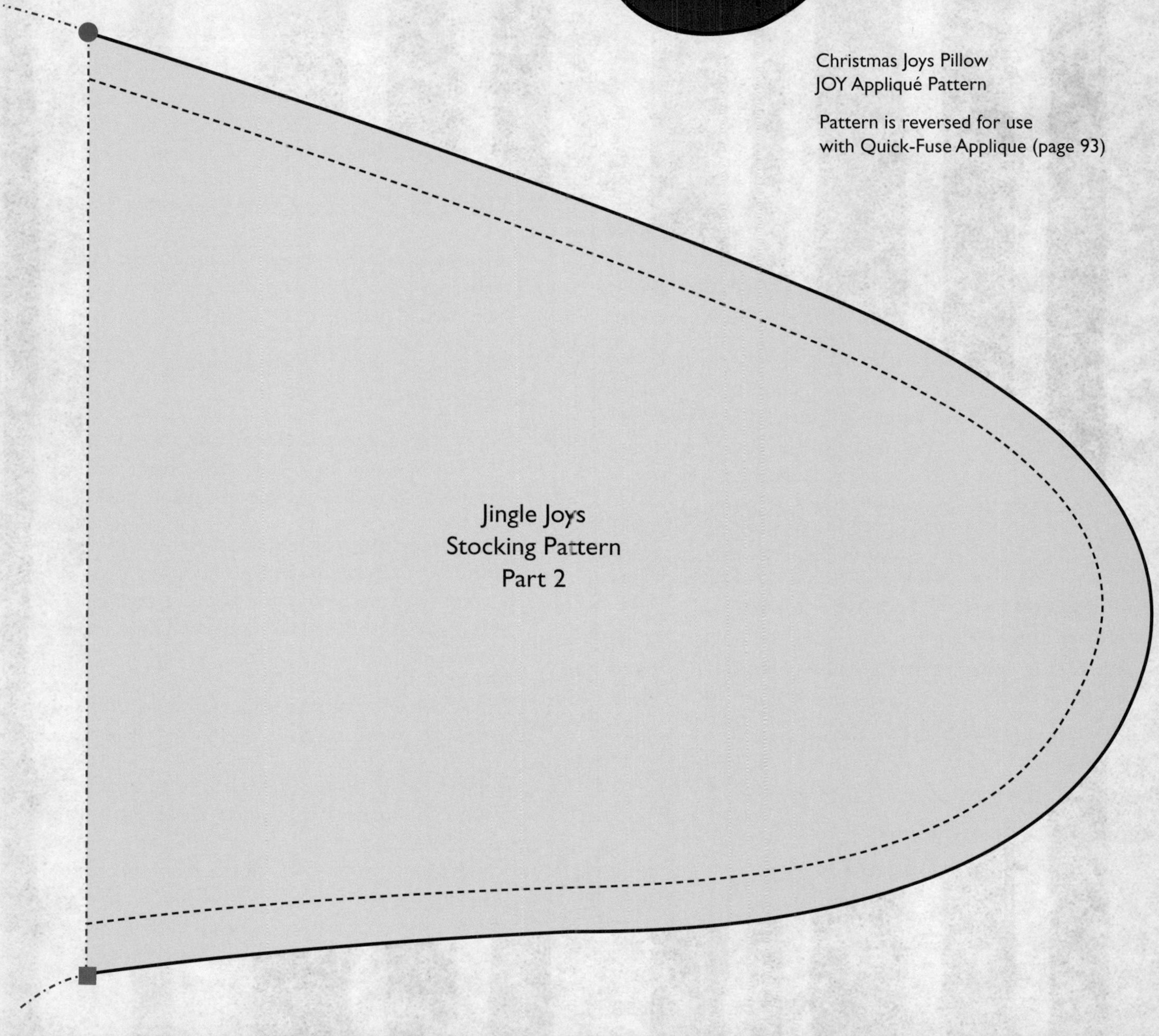

Jingle Joys
Stocking Pattern
Part 2

JOY Ornaments

GETTING STARTED

These whimsical ornaments will add a delightful extra to a package, or display several in groupings around the house. Read all instructions before beginning and use ¼"-wide seam allowance throughout.

MAKING THE ORNAMENTS

Refer to Ornament Patterns on page 45 to trace tree and pointed oval shapes onto template plastic marking placement lines. Cut on drawn lines.

TREE ORNAMENT

1. On wrong side of one 6" tree fabric square trace tree shape; this will be your sewing line. Cut approximately ¼" away from drawn line.

2. If desired sew sequin trim onto right side of marked tree fabric piece using a wide zigzag stitch or hand-stitch trim. **Option:** Hand sew or glue sequin trim to tree after construction is completed.

3. Place marked fabric right sides together with 6" tree fabric square. Sew on drawn line leaving bottom tree trunk edge free of stitching. Trim, clip, turn right side out, and press. Stuff with polyester fiberfill to desired fullness. Hand-stitch opening closed.

YOU WILL NEED...
One of Each Ornament

- **TREE ORNAMENT FABRIC - ⅛ yard**
  Two 6" Squares
- **POINTED OVAL ORNAMENT FABRIC - ⅛ yard**
  Four 3" x 5"
- **ORNAMENT ACCENT - Scrap**
  Two 2" x 5"
- **EMBROIDERY FLOSS - Lime green**
- **SEQUIN TRIM - ⅔ yard**
- **RICKRACK TRIM - ⅓ yard**
- **BEAD**
- **WIRE**
- **TEMPLATE PLASTIC**
- **POLYESTER FIBERFILL**

4. Using six strands and approximately 12" of floss, stitch a loop to ornament for hanger. Take a stitch at top tree point, pulling half of the floss length through to other side. Tie ends together to complete loop.

POINTED OVAL ORNAMENT

1. Sew one 2" x 5" Ornament Accent fabric piece between two 3" x 5" Pointed Oval fabric pieces. Press. Make two.

2. Referring to photo, arrange rickrack on center strip and stitch in place. Make two.

3. On wrong side of one pieced unit trace Pointed Oval Pattern aligning center strip seams with pattern placement lines. This will be the stitching line.

4. Place pieced units right sides together, aligning seam lines, and stitch on drawn line leaving a 3" opening for turning. Trim, clip, turn right side out, and press. Fill with polyester fiberfill to desired fullness. Hand-stitch opening closed.

5. Thread wire through top of ornament, attach bead, twist wire to secure bead, and form a hanging loop.

6. To make tassel, wrap six strands of embroidery floss around 1" square of cardboard 10-15 times. Run a needle with thread between cardboard and floss and tie section together. Slide floss off cardboard and wrap several times with a contrasting thread approximately ¼" from top to form tassel head. Run needle and thread through the end of ornament and attach tassel. Cut loops and trim to desired length.

Tree Ornament

Soft and light, quick and bright, sew a tree-full of fun fabric ornaments! Perfect for an ornament exchange or to adorn packages, these cute ornaments will inspire your creativity.

Joy Ornament Patterns

Tracing Line _____

Placement Line -·-·-·-·-·-·-·

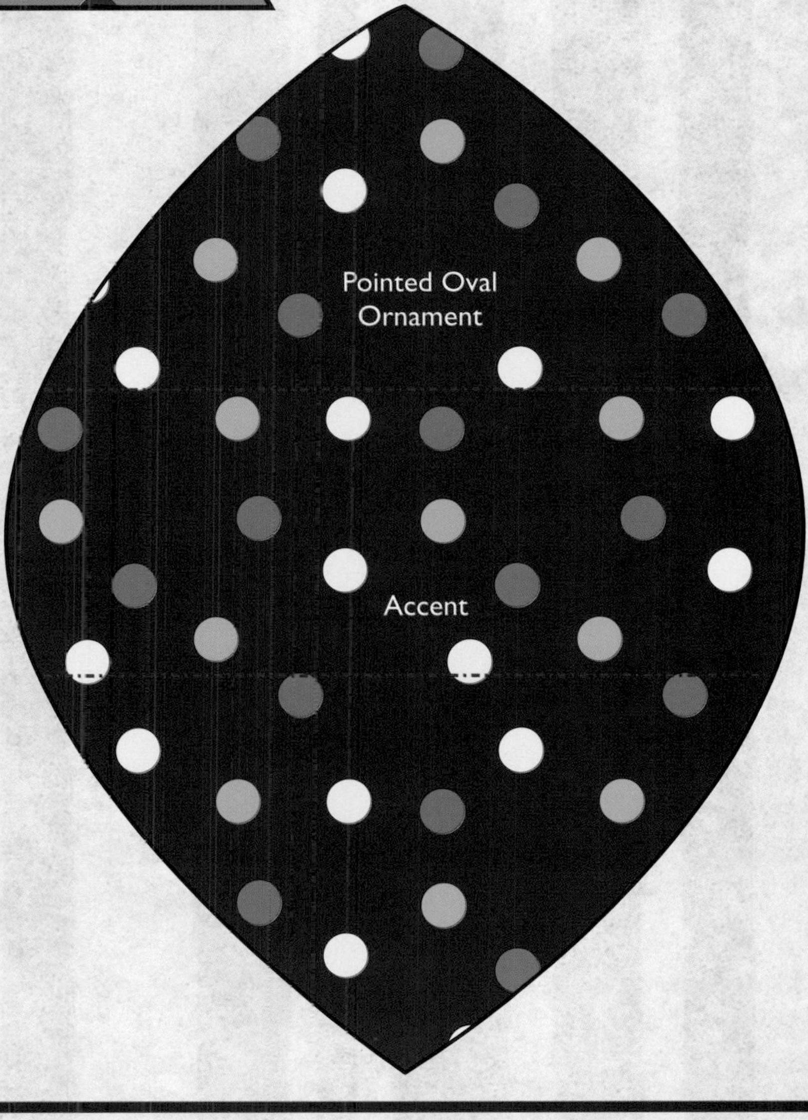

Pointed Oval Ornament

Accent

Joy, Joy, Joy
Table Runner

Read all instructions before beginning and use ¼"-wide seam allowance throughout. Read Cutting Strips and Pieces on page 92 prior to cutting fabric.

GETTING STARTED

This ensemble is fast to make and will enhance any table. Make several, changing the color palette, to decorate for different seasons. Refer to Accurate Seam Allowance on page 92. Whenever possible use the Assembly Line Method on page 92. Press seams in the direction of arrows.

Joy, Joy, Joy Table Runner Finished Size: 39" x 14"	FIRST CUT		SECOND CUT	
	Number of Strips or Pieces	Dimensions	Number of Pieces	Dimensions
Fabric A Table Runner Background ½ yard	1	14½" x 42"	1 2	14½" x 31" 14½" x 2½"
Fabric B Table Topper Background ⅓ yard	1	10" square		
Fabric C Accent Strips ½ yard* (Fussy Cut)	4 2	18" x 1¾" 14½" x 3¼"		

Backing - 1 yard
      16" x 42" piece
      14" square

Batting - 18" x 42"
      16" square

Wide Rickrack - 1 yard

Narrow Rickrack - 1⅛ yards

Sequin Trim - 1 yard

Decorative Trim - 1 yard

1" Bells - 4

*Fussy Cut from directional stripe fabric. If using non-directional fabric, reduce yardage to ¼ yard.

MAKING THE TABLE RUNNER

1. Arrange and sew together two 14½" x 2½" Fabric A strips, two 14½" x 3¼" Fabric C strips, and one 14½" x 31" Fabric A piece as shown. Press.

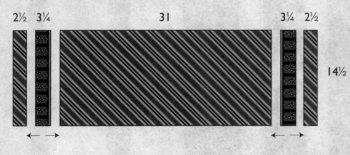

2½ 3¼   31   3¼ 2½   14½

2. Referring to photo and layout, arrange and sew decorative trim at each edge of Fabric C pieces and sequin trim, parallel to and about 1" away from decorative trim.

3. Layer and center table runner and 16" x 42" backing piece right sides together on 18" x 42" batting piece with wrong side of backing on batting. Using ¼"-wide seam, stitch around all edges, leaving a 4" opening on one short side for turning. Trim batting close to stitching and backing even with table runner edges. Clip corners, turn, and press. Hand-stitch opening closed. Machine or hand quilt as desired.

4. Measure short side of table runner. Cut two pieces of wide rickrack to this measurement plus 1". Fold wide rickrack ends under and sew to edge.
Note: We positioned rickrack so it extends past table runner ends.

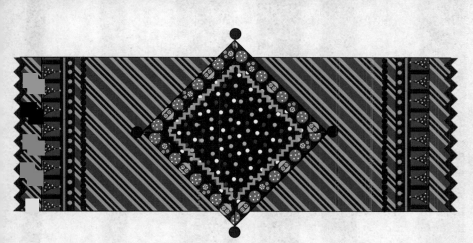

Table Runner & Table Topper Layout
39" x 14" (Table Runner)
12" Square (Table Topper)

MAKING THE TOPPER

1. Refer to Mitered Borders page 94. Sew 18" x 1¾" Fabric C strips to top, bottom, and sides of 10" Fabric B square, mitering corners. Press seams toward Fabric C.

2. Referring to photo and layout, sew narrow rickrack to center of topper ¾" away from mitered border.

3. Layer and center topper and 14" backing square right sides together, on 16" batting square, with wrong side of backing on batting piece. Stitch around all edges, leaving a 4" opening for turning. Trim batting close to stitching and backing even with topper. Clip corners, turn, and press. Hand-stitch opening closed. Machine or hand quilt as desired.

4. Sew a large bell to each corner to finish.

Express yourself! Look for fun fabrics and unusual trims to make this show-stopping table runner.

SNOW Friends

Whimsy and wonder all rolled up in a big snow ball! Lovable snowmen cavort through the holidays in this selection of quilt, craft, and decorating projects.

Snowflakes are perfect for wintertime decorating and appear on quilts, table runners, and pillows.

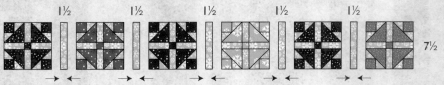

2. Sew together six Snowflake Blocks and five 1½" x 7½" Fabric A pieces as shown. Press. Make eight rows, each using a different combination of blocks.

3. Sew nine 1½" x 42" Fabric A strips together end-to-end to make one continuous 1½"-wide Fabric A strip. Cut seven 1½" x 47½" Fabric A strips.

4. Referring to photo on page 51 and layout, sew eight rows from step 2 to seven 1½" x 47½" Fabric A strips from step 3. Press toward Fabric A.

ADDING THE BORDERS

1. Sew 2" x 42" First Border strips together end-to-end to make one continuous 2"-wide First Border strip. Referring to Adding the Borders on page 94, measure quilt through center from side to side. Cut two 2"-wide First Border strips to this measurement. Sew to top and bottom of quilt. Press seams toward border.

2. Measure quilt through center from top to bottom including border just added. Cut two 2"-wide First Border strips to this measurement. Sew to sides of quilt. Press.

3. Refer to steps 1 and 2 to join, measure, trim, and sew 1¼"-wide Second Border and 3½"-wide Outside Border strips to top, bottom, and sides of quilt. Press.

LAYERING AND FINISHING

1. Cut backing crosswise into two equal pieces. Sew pieces together lengthwise to make one 64" x 80" (approximate) backing piece. Press.

2. Referring to Layering the Quilt on page 94, arrange and baste backing, batting, and top together. Hand or machine quilt as desired.

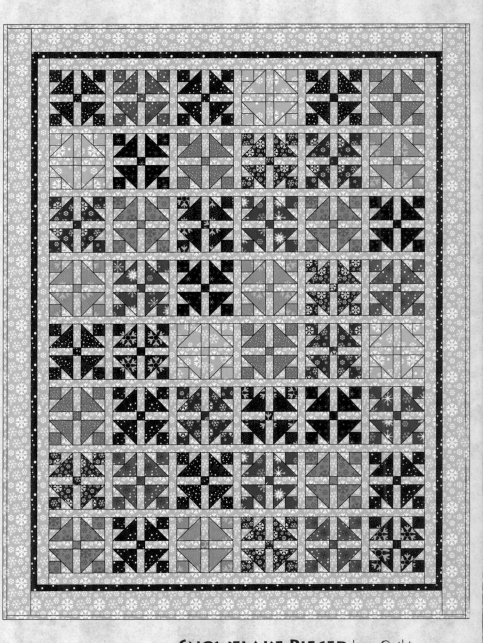

SNOWFLAKE PIECED Lap Quilt
Finished Size: 58½" x 74½"

3. Refer to Binding the Quilt on page 94. Sew 2¾" x 42" binding strips end-to-end to make one continuous 2¾"-wide binding strip. Bind quilt to finish.

EASY Fleecy Throw

Quick GIFT IDEA!

GETTING STARTED

Need a quick gift? Make this warm fleece throw personalized with a loved one's monogram initial.
Fabric Tips: Check lamé washing and ironing instructions prior to purchasing to make sure fabric can take the heat from an iron without melting. Fleece does not ravel so side edges are left unfinished. Some fleece is heat sensitive so try a quick fuse sample before starting this project.

EASY FLEECY Throw
Finished Size: 43" x 57"

Make a personal and special gift in minutes by adding a monogram, trims, and appliqués to a fun fleece throw.

MAKING THE THROW

1. Fold under 1½" along each short side of 43" x 60" Fleece piece. Stitch 1" away from folded edges to make hems.

2. Position rickrack on the right side of throw covering stitches from step 1. Stitch rickrack in place.
   Note: We elected to add trim and appliqués to one end of fleece only. If embellishments on both ends of fleece are desired, increase trim, rickrack, and appliqué fabric requirements.

3. Referring to photo, position and stitch decorative trim approximately ⅛" away from rickrack. On wrong side trim excess fabric in hem area close to stitches.

4. Select a monogram letter and font approximately 2" (50mm) tall and embroider on lamé by machine or hand. Stabilizer is recommended.

5. Refer to appliqué instructions on page 93. Use Snowflake 1 and 2 patterns on page 68 and 69 to trace snowflakes on paper side of fusible web. Fuse monogrammed lamé to center of Snowflake 1.

6. Refer to photo to position and fuse all appliqués to throw. Finish appliqué edges with machine blanket stitch or other decorative stitching as desired.
   Tip: Place stabilizer on wrong side of fleece when adding decorative stitching to prevent stretching.

YOU WILL NEED...

- **FLEECE** - 1⅛ yards (60" wide) One 43" x 60" Piece
- **SNOWFLAKE APPLIQUÉS** - ⅜ yard
- **SNOWFLAKE APPLIQUÉ CENTERS** ⅛ yard Lamé
- **LIGHTWEIGHT FUSIBLE WEB** - ½ yard
- **STABILIZER** - 1¼ yards
- **WIDE RICKRACK** - 1¼ yards
- **DECORATIVE TRIM** - 1¼ yards

SNOW FRIENDS Wall Quilt

MAKING THE QUILT

1. Sew one 14½" Fabric A square between two 1½" x 14½" Fabric D strips. Press seams toward Fabric D. Sew this unit between two 1½" x 16½" Fabric D strips as shown. Press.

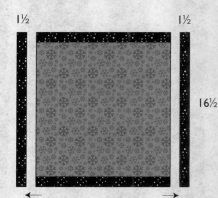

Snow Friends Wall Quilt Finished Size: 21" x 29½"	FIRST CUT		SECOND CUT	
	Number of Strips or Pieces	Dimensions	Number of Pieces	Dimensions
Fabric A Background ½ yard	1	14½" square		
Fabric B Border Triangles and Binding ⅜ yard	2	2¾" x 42" (Binding)		
	2	2½" x 42"	16	2½" x 4½"
Fabric C Border Triangles ⅜ yard	1	4" x 16"		
	3	2½" x 42"	36	2½" squares
Fabric D Accent Border and Binding ⅓ yard	2	2¾" x 42" (Binding)		
	2	1½" x 42"	2	1½" x 16½"
			2	1½" x 14½"
Fabric E Top and Bottom Border ⅓ yard	2	4¾" x 20½" "Fussy Cut"		

Backing - ¾ yard

Batting - 25" x 33½"

Snowman Appliqués - Assorted scraps, cotton and wool

Lightweight Fusible Web - ½ yard

Embroidery Floss - Silver, ivory, green, black

Assorted Sequins & Beads

Fabric Glue

FABRIC REQUIREMENTS AND CUTTING INSTRUCTIONS

Read all instructions before beginning and use ¼"-wide seam allowance throughout. Read Cutting Strips and Pieces on page 92 prior to cutting fabric.

GETTING STARTED

Our wintry pals are ready for a day of fun in this glittery snow scene. Sequins and beads add luster. Top and bottom borders were "fussy cut" to position words. Refer to Accurate Seam Allowance on page 92. Whenever possible use the Assembly Line Method on page 92. Press seams in the direction of arrows.

2. Refer to Quick Corner Triangles on page 92. Making quick corner triangle units, sew two 2½" Fabric C squares to one 2½" x 4½" Fabric B piece as shown. Press. Make sixteen.

C = 2½ x 2½
B = 2½ x 4½
Make 16

3. Sew four units from step 2 together as shown. Press. Make four.

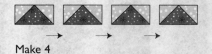

Make 4

4. Sew one unit from step 3 between two 2½" Fabric C squares as shown. Press. Make two.

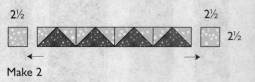

Make 2

5. Sew unit from step 1 between two units from step 3. Press toward center. Sew this unit between two units from step 4 as shown. Press.

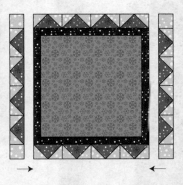

6. Sew unit from step 5 between two 4¾" x 20½" Fabric E pieces as shown. Press.

20½

4¾

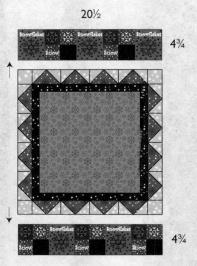

4¾

ADDING THE APPLIQUÉS

Refer to appliqué instructions on page 93. Our instructions are for Quick-Fuse Appliqué, but if you prefer hand appliqué, reverse templates and add ¼"-wide seam allowance.

1. Use patterns on pages 56 and 57 to trace Snow Friends on paper side of fusible web. Use assorted scraps to prepare all appliqués for fusing.

2. On paper-side of fusible web draw a 3½" x 13" rectangle and fuse to one 4" x 16" Fabric C piece. On one long side, cut a gentle curve to depict rolling snow mounds. Cut remaining sides on drawn line.

These whimsical characters personify the love and good will of the holiday season. Embroidered accents and a sprinkling of sequins complete this warm holiday scene.

3 Refer to photo on page 55 and layout to position and fuse appliqués to quilt. Finish appliqué edges with machine satin stitch or other decorative stitching as desired.

ADDING SPARKLE TO THE QUILT

Embellishments can be added now or after quilting is completed.

1. Refer to photo on page 55, layout, and snowflake patterns on pages 57-58. Trace three snowflakes, one of each size, to quilt using preferred method.
Tip: If using fabric that's hard to mark try this easy method. Trace snowflakes on tissue paper and pin to front of quilt. Stitch through tissue and fabric. After all stitching is completed, remove tissue paper.

2. Using six strands of silver embroidery floss, stitch each snowflake spoke using a long single stitch. Attach one sequin and bead to the center of snowflake and to each spoke's end.

3. To add extra glitter, follow manufacturer's instructions and using fabric glue, attach additional sequins to sky and ground to resemble falling snow.

4. Refer to embroidery stitch guide on page 95 and Snow Friends patterns on pages 56-57, use 2 strands of black embroidery floss to stitch French knots for eyes and mouths on snowmen.

5. Cut piece of wool scrap 1½" x 3". Fuse a ¼" x 2½" fusible web piece to top section only leaving bottom free of adhesive. Measure width of each scarf end and cut wool to this measurement, only a small amount of web is needed along top edge. Fuse to scarf, unravel wool ends to make fringe and trim to desire length. **Optional:** Refer to Embroidery Stitch Guide on page 95 and Snow Friends patterns on pages 56-57 to stitch fringe using a stem stitch and embroidery floss.

LAYERING AND FINISHING

1. Cut backing piece to measure 25" x 33½".

2. Referring to Layering the Quilt on page 94, arrange and baste backing, batting, and top together. Hand or machine quilt as desired.

3. Refer to Binding the Quilt on page 94 and bind quilt to finish. **Note:** We used two different binding fabrics, Fabric B for the top and bottom and Fabric D for the sides.

SNOW FRIENDS Wall Quilt
Finished Size: 21" x 29½"

STOCKING *Ornaments*

MAKING THE STOCKINGS

1. Refer to Stocking Pattern to cut two stockings (one regular and one reversed) from fleece scraps.

2. Embellish stocking front as desired. Our stockings were embellished as follows.

   •Blue—Refer to embroidery snowflake stitches below to mark front of stocking by preferred method. Using three strands of silver embroidery floss and a long stitch, stitch snowflake adding a crystal bead at points. Sew or glue sequins as desired.

   •Green—Using an embroidery machine, stitch the word "Snow" to cuff piece. Embroidery can be done by hand if desired. Add beads in step 3 at tips of every other blanket stitch.

   •Cream—Snowflakes buttons and sequins were arranged and stitched to stocking front.

3. Place matching stocking pieces wrong sides together. Referring to photo and Embroidery Stitch Guide on page 95, use three strands of embroidery floss to stitch a blanket stitch around outside edge of stocking leaving top free of stitches.

4. Sew 2½" x 6" or 4½" x 6½" Cuff piece short ends together. Press. Depending on the thickness of cuff fabrics use one of the following methods to attach cuff to stocking.

   •Hand stitch cuff to top of stocking.

   •Place 2½"-wide Cuff piece inside stocking with right side of cuff to wrong side of stocking, stitch using a ¼"-wide seam. Fold cuff to the right side of stocking.

   •Fold 4½"-wide Cuff piece in half lengthwise to make a 2¼"-wide piece. Place cuff inside stocking matching raw edges and stitch using ¼"-wide seam. Fold cuff to right side of stocking.

5. Fold 4" piece of cording in half, sew loop to the inside of stocking at back seam (heel side).

6. Add additional embellishments to stocking as desired. Tinsel garland was sewn to one stocking cuff and sequin trim to another.

Tiny stocking add delightful accents to trees, windows, and wreaths. Use them for gift card holders or to hold cutlery at the dining table.

YOU WILL NEED...

- **STOCKING - Assorted fleece scraps**
- **CUFF - SCRAPS**
  2½" x 6½" Berber
  4½" x 6½" Fleece
- **EMBROIDERY FLOSS**
  Silver and Blue
- **ASSORTED BEADS, BUTTONS, AND SEQUINS**
- **LIGHTWEIGHT INTERFACING**
  (Optional)
- **CORDING - ⅛ yard per Stocking**

Stocking Pattern

Tracing Line ———————
Embroidery Placement ·················

EMBROIDERED ❄ Snowman Pillow

GETTING STARTED

Use ½" seams for fleece projects. Use caution when pressing fleece.

STITCHING THE SNOWMAN

1. Using Bluework Snowman Pattern on page 61, trace or copy onto paper. Because it is hard to mark on fleece, we chose to transfer the pattern using a sewing machine.

2. Using a temporary spray adhesive and following manufacturer's instructions, center pattern onto wrong side of 8½" Fabric A square.

3. Set machine stitch length to 16-18 stitches per inch; place a light blue thread in bobbin and match top thread to fabric. Stitch around pattern following all lines. Remove paper after stitching is completed.

The joys of winter are emphasized in this pillow with its charming bluework snowman surrounded by the warmth of comfy fleece borders.

Stitch using a small stitch length on wrong side of fabric.

Bobbin thread showing on right side of fabric.

YOU WILL NEED...

- **FABRIC A (Center)** - ⅓ yard Fleece
  One 8½" square

- **FABRIC B (Border & Backing)** - ⅝ yard
  Two 11" x 16½" Pieces
  Two 4½" x 16½" Pieces
  Two 4½" x 8½" Pieces

- **BATTING** - 18" x 18"

- **LINING** - ½ yard

- **EMBROIDERY FLOSS** - Silver, dark blue & light blue

- **LIGHTWEIGHT FUSIBLE INTERFACING** ⅝ yard

- **LIGHT BLUE THREAD FOR BOBBIN**

- **TEMPORARY FABRIC ADHESIVE SPRAY**

- **16" PILLOW FORM**

- **BLUE SEED BEADS**

4. Refer to Embroidery Guide on page 95. Using
   four strands of light blue embroidery floss and
   a small running or quilting stitch, follow previous
   machine stitching lines to stitch vest area only.

5. Using four strands of dark blue embroidery
   floss and a small running or quilting stitch,
   stitch all other snowman elements. Make French
   Knots for snowman eyes and mouth.

Right side of
fabric after
embroidery is
completed.

6. To make hat pom-pom, wrap six strands of
   embroidery floss around pencil 10-15 times. Run a
   threaded needle between pencil and floss and tie
   section together. Slide floss off pencil and stitch to
   hat. Cut loops, separate thread to fringe, and trim to
   desired length.

7. Use six strands of silver embroidery floss to stitch
   snowflake. Attach blue seed beads to ends of each
   spoke.

Making the Pillow

1. Following manufacturer's directions cut and press
   lightweight fusible interfacing to the wrong side of all
   Fabric B pieces to prevent fleece from stretching.

2. Sew embroidered Fabric A square between two
   4½" x 8½" Fabric B pieces. Press seams toward
   Fabric B. Sew this unit between two 4½" x 16½"
   Fabric B pieces. Press.

3. Referring to Finishing Pillows on page 95, step 1, to
   prepare pillow top for quilting. Quilt as desired.

4. Use two 11" x 16½" backing pieces and refer to
   Finishing Pillows, page 95, steps 2-4, to sew backing.
   Insert 16" pillow form or refer to Pillow Forms page
   95 to make a pillow form if desired.

SNOWFLAKE
Placemat & Table Runner

Decorate your wintertime table with an avalanche of fabric snowflakes. These easy placemats and table runner will make a snowy statement all winter long. Make as many placemats as you need—our fabric requirements are for one placemat.

MAKING THE PLACEMAT

1. Refer to appliqué instructions on page 93. Our instructions are for Quick-Fuse Appliqué. Use patterns on pages 66, 67, and 68 to trace one each of Snowflake Table Runner patterns #1, #3, and #4 on paper side of fusible web. Use WoolFelt to prepare all appliqués for fusing.

2. Refer to photo to position and fuse appliqués to 14½" x 18½" Background piece.

3. Referring to photo, outline and add dots to snowflakes, using Twinkles® Writer and following manufacturer's instructions.

4. Layer and center unit from step 3 and 16" x 20" backing piece right sides together on batting, wrong side of backing on batting. Using ¼"-wide seam, stitch around all edges, leaving a 4" opening on one side for turning. Trim batting close to stitching and backing even with placemat edges. Clip corners, turn, and press. Hand-stitch opening closed.

5. Referring to photo, arrange and sew rickrack to all sides. Arrange and sew trim approximately ⅛" away from rickrack inside edge.

YOU WILL NEED...
For One Placemat

- **BACKGROUND** - ½ yard Cotton
  One 14½" x 18½" piece
- **BACKING** - ½ yard
  One 16" x 20" piece
- **BATTING** - 16" x 20"
- **SNOWFLAKE APPLIQUÉS** - ⅓ yard WoolFelt™
- **HEAVYWEIGHT FUSIBLE WEB** - ⅓ yard
- **WIDE WHITE CHENILLE RICKRACK** - 1⅞ yards
- **NARROW SILVER TRIM** - 1⅞ yards
- **DECOART® TWINKLES® WRITER** - Silver

Note: Placemats are not washable unless appliqué edges are finished and WoolFelt is pre-washed.

Frosty snowflakes are frozen in time on this quick and easy table runner and placemats ensemble. WoolFelt appliqués don't require any stitching and silver glitter adds holiday glitz.

SNOWFLAKE Placemat Finished Size: 14" x 18"

Making the Table Runner

1. Measure short side of 16½" x 45½" Table Runner Background piece to find center and mark. Measure 8¼" on each corner as shown. Align ruler to draw, cut, and remove triangle section to form a point on each end.

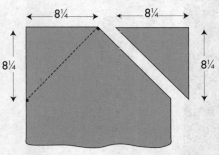

2. Refer to appliqué instructions on page 93. Our instructions are for Quick-Fuse Appliqué. Use patterns on pages 66, 67, and 68 to trace two each of Snowflake Table Runner patterns #1, #2, and #3 and one each of #4 and #5 on paper side of fusible web. Use WoolFelt to prepare all appliqués for fusing.

3. Position and fuse appliqués to fabric as desired. WoolFelt appliqués do not ravel, so stitching edges is optional.

4. Referring to photo, outline and add dots to snowflakes using Twinkles® Writer and following manufacturer's instructions.

5. Layer and center table runner and 20" x 49" backing piece right sides together on batting, wrong side of backing on batting. Using ¼"-wide seam, stitch around all edges, leaving a 4" opening on one side for turning. Trim batting close to stitching and backing even with Table Runner edges. Clip corners, turn, and press. Hand-stitch opening closed.

6. Referring to photo, arrange and sew rickrack to table runner, half of rickrack will extend past fabric edge. Arrange and sew silver trim to table runner or embellish with decorative stitching.

You Will Need...
For Table Runner

- **BACKGROUND** - 1⅜ yards Cotton
  One 16½" x 45½"
- **BACKING** - 1⅜ yards
  One 20" x 49"
- **BATTING** - 20" x 49"
- **SNOWFLAKE APPLIQUÉS** - ⅔ yard WoolFelt™
- **LIGHTWEIGHT FUSIBLE WEB** - 1 yard
- **WIDE WHITE CHENILLE RICKRACK** - 3½ yards
- **NARROW SILVER TRIM** - 3½ yards
- **DECOART® TWINKLES® WRITER** - Silver

SNOWFLAKE Table Runner Finished Size: 16" x 45"

Snowflake Table Runner
Patterns for Quick-Fuse Applique (page 93)

Tracing Line _____

Tracing Line ------------------------

(will be hidden behind other fabrics)

Placement Line _.._.._.._.._.._.._..

Snowflake
Table Runner
Pattern #3

Make 2

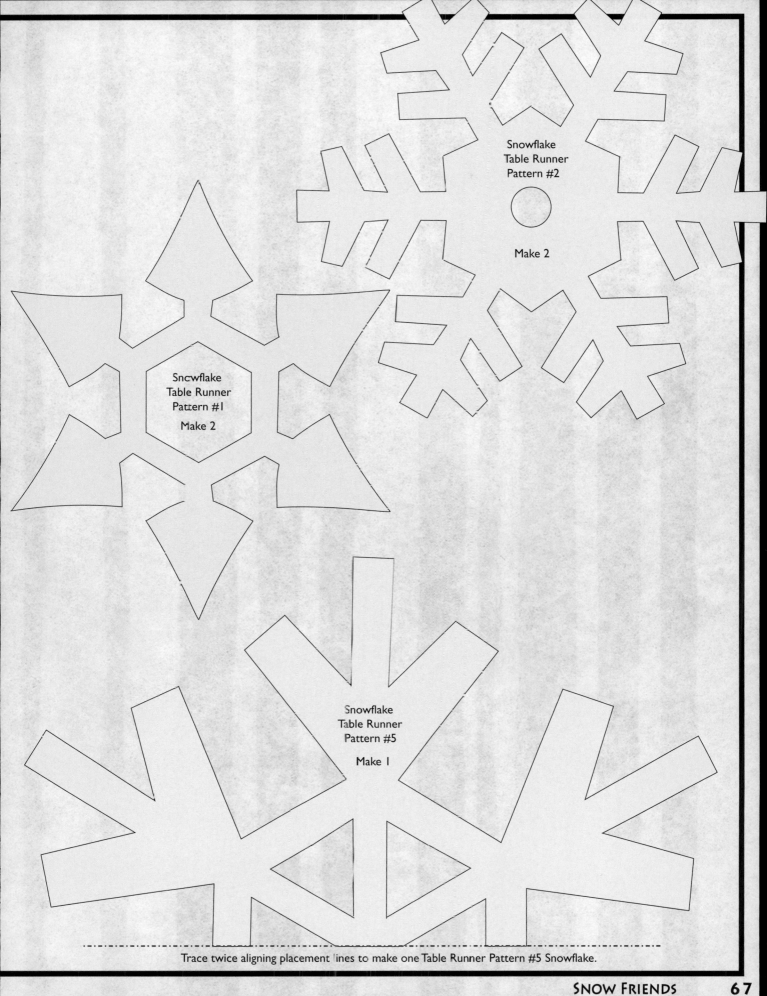

Snowflake
Table Runner
Pattern #2

Make 2

Snowflake
Table Runner
Pattern #1

Make 2

Snowflake
Table Runner
Pattern #5

Make 1

Trace twice aligning placement lines to make one Table Runner Pattern #5 Snowflake.

Easy Fleecy Throw
Pattern #1
Make 1

Joy Joy Joy

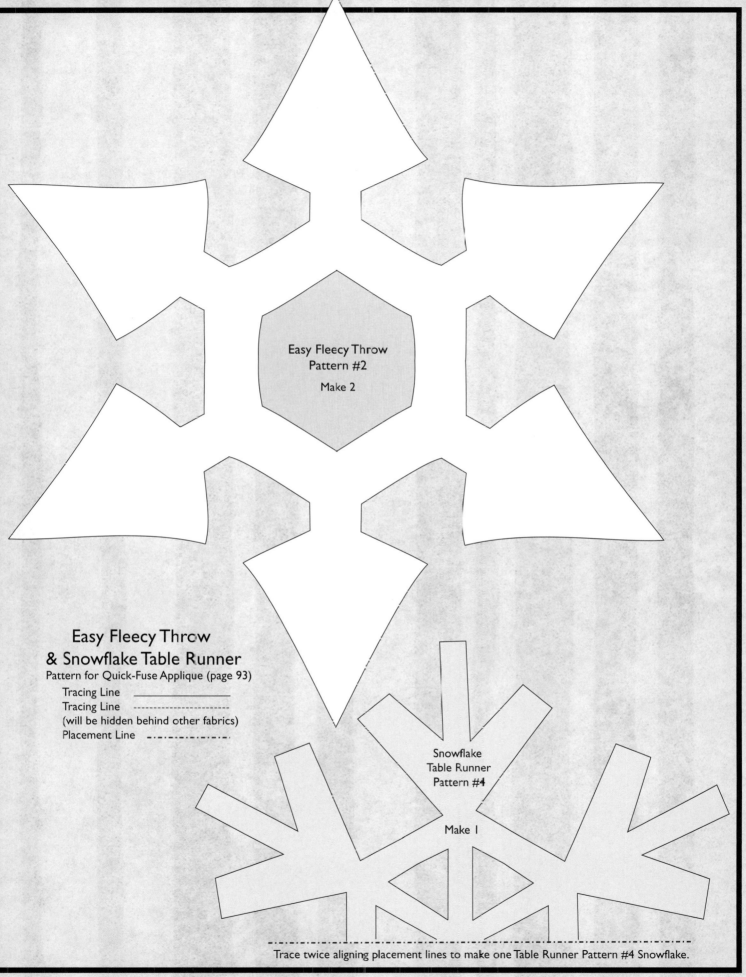

Easy Fleecy Throw
Pattern #2

Make 2

Easy Fleecy Throw
& Snowflake Table Runner
Pattern for Quick-Fuse Applique (page 93)

Tracing Line ——————————
Tracing Line - - - - - - - - - - - -
(will be hidden behind other fabrics)
Placement Line - · - · - · - · - · -

Snowflake
Table Runner
Pattern #4

Make 1

Trace twice aligning placement lines to make one Table Runner Pattern #4 Snowflake.

HoLiday HOMES

Celebrate a traditional holiday filled with all the warmth and joys of home with this charming assortment of quilt and decorating projects.

Pieced houses, old world Santas and poinsettias are the symbols of the season in this assortment of sophisticated, traditional projects.

HOLIDAY HOMES
Wall Quilt

Holiday Homes Wall Quilt Finished Size: 43" x 43"	FIRST CUT		SECOND CUT	
	Number of Strips or Pieces	Dimensions	Number of Pieces	Dimensions
See chart at right for Fabrics A - G				
Fabric H Block Accent and Block Border ⅙ yard	2	2" x 42"	1	2" x 22"
			1	2" x 19"
			1	2" square
	1	1" x 42"	1	1" x 19"
			2	1" x 9½"
Fabric I Block Border ⅙ yard	2	2" x 42"	1	2" x 22"
			1	2" x 19"
			1	2" square
Fabric K Tree Border Background ⅝ yard	2	4½" x 42"	4	4½" x 7"
			4	4½" x 6"
	2	2½" x 42"	24	2½" squares
	2	2¼" x 42"	8	2¼" x 6½"
			8	2" squares
Fabric L ¼ yard Tree Branches	2	2½" x 42"	12	2½" x 4½"
	1	1" x 42"	4	1" x 6½"
Fabric M Scrap Tree Trunk	4	1½" x 2"		
Fabric N ¼ yard Accent Border	4	1¾" x 42"	2	1¾" x 32½"
			2	1¾" x 30"
Fabric O - Border ¼ yard each of 7 fabrics	3*	1½" x 42" (*Cut for each of 5 fabrics)		
	4*	1½" x 42" (*Cut for each of 2 fabrics)		
Fabric P - Border ⅛ yard each of 7 fabrics	7*	1½" x 42" (*Cut one strip from each of 7 fabrics)		
Fabric Q ⅛ yard Star	2	1½" x 42"	32	1½" squares
Fabric R Star Background ⅙ yard	1	2½" x 42"	4	2½" squares
			16	2½" x 1½"
	1	1½" x 42"	16	1½" squares
Fabric S ⅙ yard Wool Accent	4	4½" squares		
Binding ½ yard	5	2¾" x 42"		

Backing - 2¾ yards
Batting - 49" x 49"

Four 1" Buttons
Template Plastic

FABRIC REQUIREMENTS AND CUTTING INSTRUCTIONS

Read all instructions before beginning and use ¼"-wide seam allowance throughout. Read Cutting Strips and Pieces on page 92 prior to cutting fabric.

GETTING STARTED

This winsome wall quilt can be featured in your home all year long. It's constructed with several different techniques – pieced blocks, strip sets, and dimensional accents – all of which add interest to this art piece. Refer to Accurate Seam Allowance on page 92. Whenever possible use the Assembly Line Method on page 92. Press seams in the direction of arrows.

MAKING THE HOUSE BLOCK

1. Sew together two 1½" x 3" Fabric A pieces, two 1½" Fabric B squares, and one 1½" x 2½" Fabric A piece as shown.

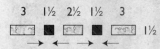

2. Draw a 45 degree angle on the wrong side of one 3" x 7" Fabric D piece as shown. Place marked piece, right sides together, with 3" x 5½" Fabric C piece, noting angle and fabric placement. Stitch on drawn line, trim ¼" away from stitching and press. Piece should measure 3" x 9½".

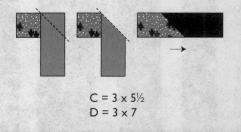

C = 3 x 5½
D = 3 x 7

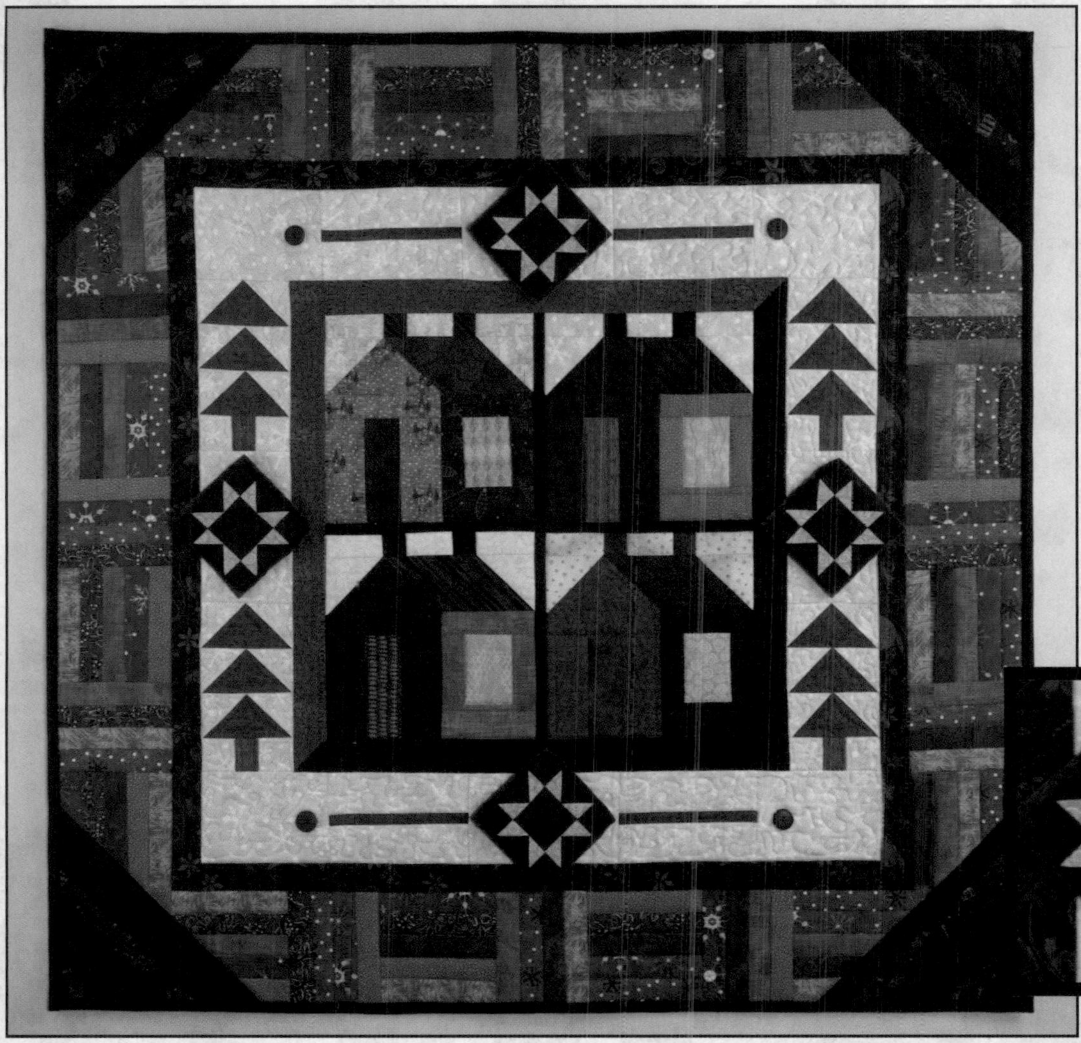

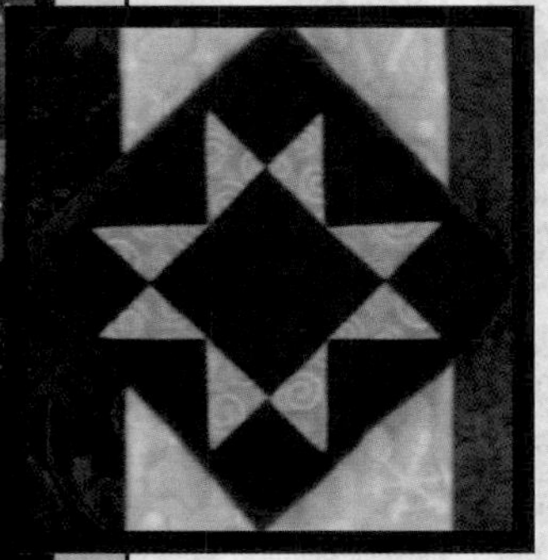

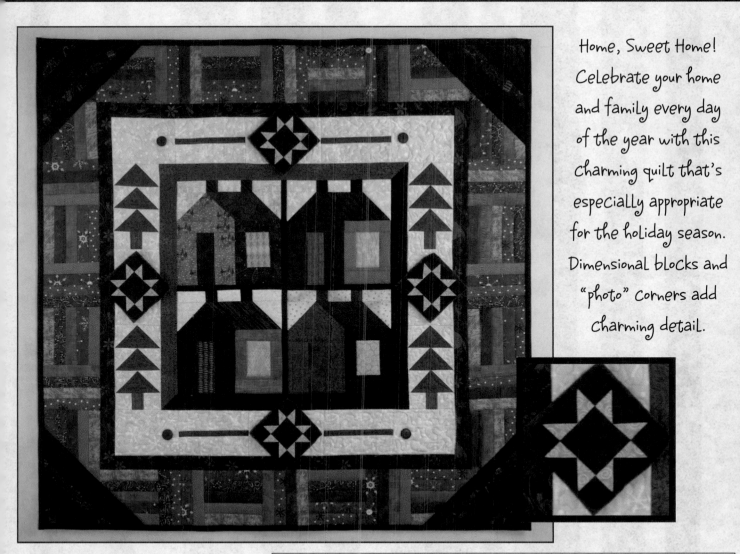

Home, Sweet Home! Celebrate your home and family every day of the year with this charming quilt that's especially appropriate for the holiday season. Dimensional blocks and "photo" corners add charming detail.

3. Refer to Quick Corner Triangles on page 92. Making quick corner triangle units, sew two 3' Fabric A squares to unit from step 2 as shown. Press.

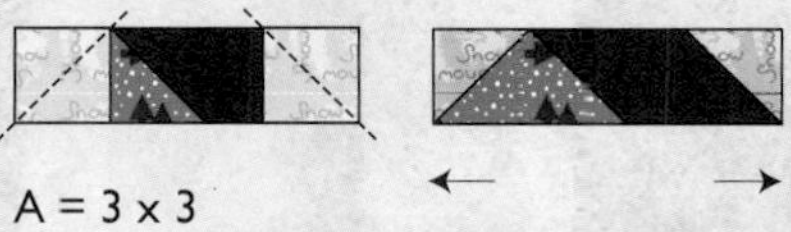

A = 3 x 3
Unit from step 2

4. Sew 1½" x 5½" Fabric C piece to 1½" x 4½" Fabric E piece as shown. Press.

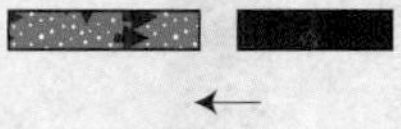

House Blocks For Wall Quilt & Bed Quilt (page 78)	WALL QUILT (Four Blocks)			BED QUILT (Six Blocks)		
	Yardage	Number of Strips or Pieces	Dimensions	Yardage	Number of Strips or Pieces	Dimensions
Fabric A House Background	⅛ yard*	2* 2* 1*	3" squares 1½" x 3" 1½" x 2½"	⅛ yard**	6** 6** 3**	3" squares 1½" x 3" 1½" x 2½"
Fabric B Chimney	Scrap*	2*	1½" squares		6**	1½" squares
Fabric C House Front	⅛ yard*	1* 2* 1*	3" x 5½" 2¼" x 5" 1½" x 5½"	¼ yard**	3** 6** 3**	3" x 5½" 2¼" x 5" 1½" x 5½"
Fabric D Roof	Scrap*	1*	3" x 7"	⅛ yard**	3**	3" x 7"
Fabric E House Side	⅛ yard*	1* 1* 2*	2" x 4½" 1½" x 4½" 1½" x 3½"	⅙ yard**	3** 3** 6**	2" x 4½" 1½" x 4½" 1½" x 3½"
Fabric F Door	Scrap*	1*	2" x 5"	⅛ yard**	3**	2" x 5"
Fabric G Window	Scrap*	1*	2½" x 3½"	⅛ yard**	3**	2½" x 3½"
	*Cut each from four fabrics			**Cut each from two fabrics		

5. Sew one 2" x 5" Fabric F piece between two 2¼" x 5" Fabric C pieces as shown. Press.

2¼ 2 2¼

5

6. Sew one 2½" x 3½" Fabric G piece between two 1½" x 3½" Fabric E pieces as shown. Press. Sew this unit to one 2" x 4½" Fabric E piece. Press.

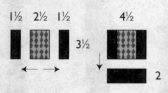

1½ 2½ 1½   4½

3½

2

7. Sew unit from step 5 to unit from step 6 as shown. Press.

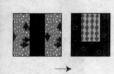

8. Arrange and sew together units from steps 1, 3, 4, and 7 as shown. Press. House Block measures 9½" square. Refer to steps 1-7 to make four blocks, one of each combination, for Holiday Homes Wall Quilt.

House Block

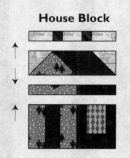

Block measures 9½" square
Make 4 for wall quilt
(1 of each variation)
[For bed quilt Make 6,
3 of each combination]

HOLIDAY HOMES
Wall Quilt
Finished Size: 43" x 43"

MAKING THE WALL QUILT

1. Sew one 1" x 9½" Fabric H strip between two house blocks. Press. Make two. Sew one 1" x 19" Fabric H strip between two of these units as shown. Press.

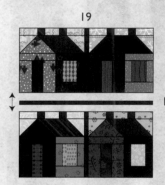

19

1

2. Refer to Quick Corner Triangles on page 92. Making a quick corner triangle unit, sew one 2" Fabric I square to one 2" x 22" Fabric H strip as shown. Press. Make two, one using 2" Fabric H square and one 2" x 22" Fabric I strip.

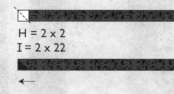

H = 2 x 2
I = 2 x 22

I = 2 x 2
H = 2 x 22

3. Sew unit from step 1 between one 2" x 19" Fabric I strip and one 2" x 19" Fabric H strip. Press. Sew this unit between units from step 2 as shown. Press.

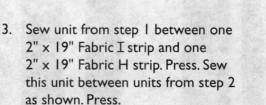

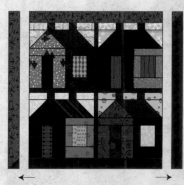

4. Making quick corner triangle units, sew two 2½" Fabric K squares to one 2½" x 4½" Fabric L piece as shown. Press. Make twelve. Sew three of these units together as shown. Press. Make four.

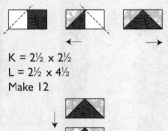

K = 2½ x 2½
L = 2½ x 4½
Make 12

Make 4

5. Sew one 1½" x 2" Fabric M piece between two 2" Fabric K squares as shown. Press. Sew one unit from step 5 to unit from this step as shown. Press. Make four.

2 1½ 2

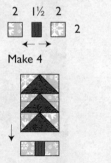 2

Make 4

Make 4
Block measures 4½" x 8"

6. Sew one 4½" x 7" Fabric K piece between two units from step 5 as shown. Press. Make two. Referring to photo on page 73 and layout on page 74, sew units to side of quilt. Press.

7

 4½

Make 2

7. Sew one 1" x 6½" Fabric L piece between two 2¼" x 6½" Fabric K pieces as shown. Press. Make four.

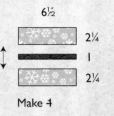

6½

2¼

1

2¼

Make 4

8. Sew together two 4½" x 6" Fabric K pieces, two units from step 7, and one 4½" x 7½" Fabric K piece as shown. Press. Make two. Sew units to top and bottom of quilt. Press.

6   7   6

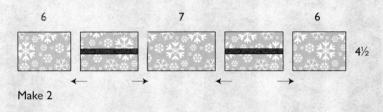 4½

Make 2

9. Sew 1¾" x 32½" Fabric N strips to top and bottom of quilt. Press seams toward Fabric N.

10. Sew 1¾" x 30" Fabric N strips to sides of quilt. Press.

11. Arrange and sew five different 1½" x 42" Fabric O strips lengthwise to make 5½" x 42" strip set. Press. Make three, each with a different fabric combination. Cut strip sets into twenty 5½"-wide segments as shown.

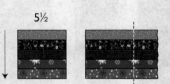

5½

Make 3 strip sets
(each using a different combination)
Cut 20 segments

12. Arrange and sew four different 1½" x 42" Fabric O strips lengthwise to make 4½" x 42" strip set. Press. Make two, each with a different fabric combination. Cut strip sets into twelve 5½"-wide segments as shown.

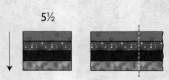

5½

Make 2 strip sets
(each using a different combination)
Cut 12 segments

13. Arrange and sew together four units from step 11 and three units from step 12 as shown. Press. Make four. Sew two to top and bottom of quilt. Press.

5½   4½   5½   4½   5½   4½   5½

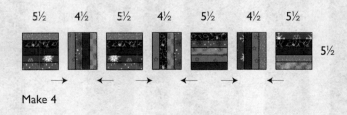 5½

Make 4

14. Sew one unit from step 13 between two segments from step 11. Press. Make two. Sew units to sides of quilt. Press.

15. Arrange and sew seven different 1½" x 42" Fabric P strips lengthwise to make 7½" x 42" strip set. Press.

16. From template plastic cut one 9½" square, then cut once diagonally to make triangle pattern piece. Align long triangle edge on strip set from step 15 along outside raw edge. Cut one triangle, flip template over and align on other outside edge to cut a second triangle as shown. Repeat process to cut four triangle units.

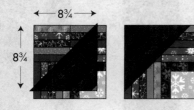

17. Referring to diagram below, measure 8¾" from corner as shown. Using temporary fabric marker, draw a diagonal line from these points, this will be triangle strip set placement line. The stitching line is 9¼" from corner and excess triangle points should extend beyond quilt raw edges at this point as shown. Using ¼"-wide seam, sew triangles to quilt top as positioned. Trim ¼" away from stitch line to complete quilt top. Press.

Layering and Finishing the Quilt

1. Cut backing crosswise into two equal pieces. Sew pieces together lengthwise to make one 49" x 80" (approximate) backing piece. Press and trim to 49" x 49". Cut four 4½" squares from trimmings.

2. Referring to Layering the Quilt on page 94, arrange and baste backing, batting and top together. Hand or machine quilt as desired.

3. Refer to Binding the Quilt on page 94. Sew 2¾" x 42" binding strips end-to-end to make one continuous 2¾"-wide binding strip. Bind quilt to finish.

4. Refer to Quick Corner Triangles on page 92. Making quick corner triangle units, sew two 1½" Fabric Q squares to one 2½" x 1½" Fabric R piece as shown. Press. Make sixteen.

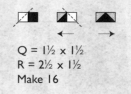

Q = 1½ x 1½
R = 2½ x 1½
Make 16

5. Sew one 2½" Fabric R square between two units from step 1 as shown. Press. Make four.

Unit A

2½

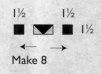

2½

Make 4

6. Sew one unit from step 1 between two 1½" Fabric R squares as shown. Press. Make eight.

1½   1½

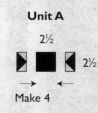

1½

Make 8

7. Sew one unit from step 2 between two of units from step 6 as shown. Press. Make four.

Make 4

8. Layer unit from step 7 and 4½" backing square, right sides together, on batting, wrong side of pieced unit on batting. Using ¼"-wide seam, stitch around all edges and trim batting close to stitching. Clip corners and cut a slit in backing piece, being careful not to cut the block, turn, stitch opening closed, and press. Quilt block as desired. Center and sew block on wool 4½" square. Make four.

9. Referring to photo on page 73 and layout on page 74, stitch Star Block and four buttons to quilt.

HOME SWEET Home

YOU WILL NEED...

- **WOODEN BLOCKS**
  6¼" x 2½" x 1½" deep
  5" x 2¾" x 1½" deep
  3¼" x 3½" x 1½" deep
- **WOOD PIECE - ½" x ½" x 17"**
  Cut into: 7", 6", 3¾" pieces
- **¼" PLYWOOD SCRAP**
  Cut into tree shape 4½" high
  and 2½" at base
- **WOOD GLUE**
- **AMERICANA® ACRYLIC CRAFT PAINTS**
  Avocado, buttermilk, antique gold, black
- **DELTA CERAMCOAT® ACRYLIC CRAFT PAINTS**
  Opaque red, autumn brown,
  dark burnt umber
- **CLEAR GLAZE**
- **MATTE SPRAY VARNISH**
- **STENCIL WITH ½" SQUARES**
- **STENCIL BRUSH**
- **ASSORTED BEADS AND BEADING WIRE**
- **HOT GLUE GUN AND LOW TEMPERATURE GLUE STICKS**
- **SCOTCH® MAGIC™ TAPE**

1. Use a table saw to shape the top of each block into a roof shape. Sand all wood pieces and remove residue. Paint each roof black. Paint ½" x ½" chimney pieces black. Allow to dry.
2. Paint body of each house (all sides) making one buttermilk, one opaque red, and one avocado. Paint tree shape with avocado paint. Allow to dry.
3. Determine the size of door for each house. Use Scotch® Magic™ Tape to mask off area around each door. Rub edges of tape to make sure they are securely adhered. Paint each door either autumn brown or dark burnt umber. Allow to dry. Remove tape.
4. Using stencil and brush, paint square windows on houses where desired.
5. Sand edges of houses, chimneys, and tree for a distressed look. Use wood glue to adhere chimneys and tree to houses and allow to dry.
6. Spray houses with matte varnish and allow to dry.
7. Mix a small amount of autumn brown paint with clear glaze. Apply glaze to houses, wiping glaze off with a clean rag until desired color is achieved. Allow to dry. Spray with matte varnish.
8. If desired, add bead embellishments. Use hot glue gun to affix small red beads to tree. String green beads and a few red beads on thin wire and form into a wreath shape, twisting ends tightly. Glue to red house door with hot glue. String clear and red beads on thin wire and form into a garland for green house. Adhere with hot glue.

These little houses will add a touch of holiday charm to a mantel or shelf. Make three this year and add a new house each year!

HOLIDAY HOMES
Bed Quilt

FABRIC REQUIREMENTS AND CUTTING INSTRUCTIONS

Read all instructions before beginning and use ¼"-wide seam allowance throughout. Read Cutting Strips and Pieces on page 92 prior to cutting fabric.

Note: Refer to chart on page 73 for House Block fabric requirements

Holiday Homes Bed Quilt Finished Size: 75" x 86"	FIRST CUT		SECOND CUT	
	Number of Strips or Pieces	Dimensions	Number of Pieces	Dimensions
This chart does not include house blocks.				
Fabric A 2⅔ yards Background & First Border	7	11½" x 42"	13	11½" squares
			10	11½" x 6"
	7	1¾" x 42"		
Fabric B ⅜ yard Block Borders & Corners	7	1½" x 42"	24	1½" x 9½"
			24	1½" squares
Fabric C ⅜ yard 9-Patch Block Accent Border	7	1½" x 42"	24	1½" x 9½"
			24	1½" squares
Fabric D ¼ yard 9-Patch	2	3" x 42"		
Fabric E ⅙ yard 9-Patch Center	1	4½" x 42"		
Fabric F ⅜ yard 9-Patch	1	4½" x 42"		
	2	3" x 42"		
Fabric G ⅜ yard Red Stars	2	6" x 42"	8	6" squares
Fabric H ⅜ yard Red Stars	2	6" x 42"	8	6" squares
Fabric I ⅜ yard Red Stars	2	6" x 42"	8	6" squares
Fabric J ⅜ yard Green Stars	2	6" x 42"	8	6" squares
Fabric K ⅜ yard Green Stars	2	6" x 42"	8	6" squares
Fabric L ⅜ yard Green Stars	2	6" x 42"	8	6" squares
BORDERS				
Second Border ⅓ yard	7	1¼" x 42"		
Third Border ⅝ yard	7	2½" x 42"		
Outside Border 1½ yards	8	6" x 42"		
Binding ¾ yard	9	2¾" x 42"		
Backing - 7 yards		Batting - 83" x 94"		

GETTING STARTED

Carolers' voices swell in sweet song as they travel throughout the neighborhood; friends and relatives sharing holiday spirit, food, and song in the warmth of a loved one's home. Bring the sweet memories of days past with this quilt. Quilt features four different 11½" square blocks (unfinished) and 11½" x 6" blocks (unfinished) showcasing stars and homes. **Note:** The house blocks are constructed first using cutting chart on page 73. Refer to Accurate Seam Allowance on page 92. Whenever possible use the Assembly Line Method on page 92. Press seams in the direction of arrows.

MAKING THE HOUSE BLOCKS (BLOCK 1)

House Block yardage and cutting chart are on page 73.

1. Refer to Holiday Homes Wall Quilt on pages 72-74, steps 1-8, for House Block instructions. Make six, three of each house combination.

2. Sew one House Block between two 1½" x 9½" Fabric B pieces. Press. Make six, three of each house combinations.

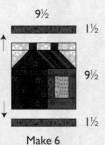

9½
1½
9½
1½

Make 6

3. Sew one 1½" x 9½" Fabric B piece between two 1½" Fabric C squares as shown. Press. Make twelve. Sew one unit from step 2 between two of these units as shown. Press and label Block 1. Make six, three of each combination. Block 1 measures 11½" square.

1½   9½   1½
                1½

Make 12

Block 1

Make 6
Block measures 11½" square

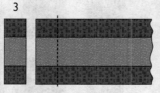

Feel right at home with this cozy neighborhood of houses. This quilt is perfect on your bed top during the holidays or any day.

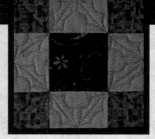

MAKING BLOCK 2

1. Sew 4½" x 42" Fabric F strip between two 3" x 42" Fabric D strips. Press seams away from center. Cut strip set into twelve 3"-wide segments as shown.

3

Cut 12 segments

2. Sew one 4½" x 42" Fabric E strip between two 3" x 42" Fabric F strips. Press seams toward center. Cut strip set into six 4½"-wide segments.

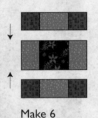

4½

Cut 6 segments

3. Sew one segment from step 2 between two segments from step 1 as shown. Press. Make six.

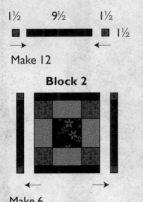

Make 6

4. Sew unit from step 3 between two 1½" x 9½" Fabric C pieces. Press seams toward Fabric C. Make six. Sew one 1½" x 9½" Fabric C piece between two 1½" Fabric B squares as shown. Press. Make twelve. Sew to sides of one unit as shown. Press and label Block 2. Make six. Block measures 11½" square.

1½   9½   1½
                1½

Make 12

Block 2

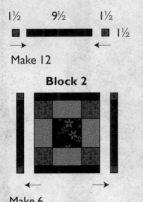

Make 6
Block measures 11½" square

Making Blocks 3, 4 and 5

1. Refer to Quick Corner Triangles on page 92. Making quick corner triangle units, sew two 6" Fabric J squares and two 6" Fabric H squares to one 11½" Fabric A square as shown. Press and label Block 3. Make seven, one each of the following fabric combinations: J/H/A, J/G/A, H/K/A, G/K/A, G/L/A, K/I/A, and L/I/A.

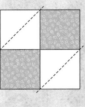

J = 6 x 6
H = 6 x 6
A = 11½ x 11½

Block 3

Make 7
(1 of each combination)

J/G/A   H/K/A   G/K/A

G/L/A   K/I/A   L/I/A

Blocks measure 11½" square

2. Making quick corner triangle units, sew two 6" Fabric J squares to one 11½" Fabric A square as shown. Press and label Block 4. Make six, one each of the following fabric combinations J/A, H/A, G/A, K/A, L/A, and I/A. Block measures 11½" square.

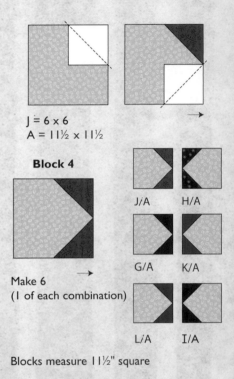

J = 6 x 6
A = 11½ x 11½

Block 4

J/A   H/A

G/A   K/A

Make 6
(1 of each combination)

L/A   I/A

Blocks measure 11½" square

3. Making quick corner triangle units, sew two 6" Fabric J squares to one 11½" x 6" Fabric A piece as shown. Press and label Block 5. Make six, one each of the following fabric combinations: J/A, H/A, L/A, and I/A. Block measures 11½" x 6".

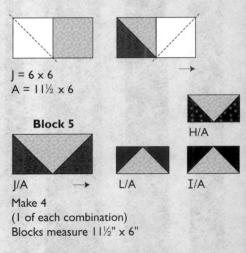

J = 6 x 6
A = 11½ x 6

Block 5

H/A

J/A   →   L/A   I/A

Make 4
(1 of each combination)
Blocks measure 11½" x 6"

ASSEMBLY

Arrange all blocks and background pieces prior to sewing to match star points for each house setting. Refer to photo on page 79 and layout. When sewing blocks into rows press seams in one direction, alternating direction from row to row.

1. Arrange and sew together three 11½" x 6" Fabric A pieces and two of Block 5 (J/A and H/A fabric combination) as shown. Press and label Row 1. Repeat step using Block 5 L/A and I/A fabric combination to make Row 7.

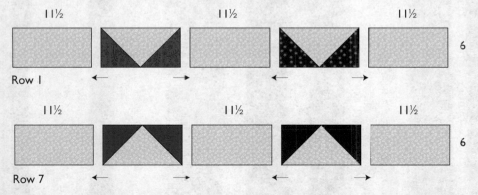

2. Referring to photo on page 79 and layout, arrange and sew together two of Block 4 (J/A and H/A) two of Block 1, and one Block 3 (J/H/A). Press. Make three rows, one row using Block 4 (G/A and K/A) and Block 3 (G/K/A) and one row using Block 4 (L/A and I/A) and Block 3 (L/I/A). Label Rows 2, 4, and 6.

HOLIDAY HOMES Bed Quilt
Finished Size: 75" x 86"

3. Referring to photo on page 79 and layout, arrange and sew together three of Block 2 and two of Block 3 (J/G/A and H/K/A). Press and label Row 3. Make Row 5 using Block 3 G/L/A and K/I/A and three of Block 2 combinations. Label Row 5.

4. Referring to photo on page 79 and layout, arrange and sew together Rows 1-7. Press.

ADDING THE BORDERS

1. Sew 1¾" x 42" First Border strips together end-to-end to make one continuous 1¾"-wide First Border strip. Referring to Adding the Borders on page 94, measure quilt through center from side to side. Cut two 1¾"-wide First Border strips to this measurement. Sew to top and bottom of quilt. Press seams toward border.

2. Measure quilt through center from top to bottom including borders just added. Cut two 1¾"-wide First Border strips to this measurement. Sew to sides of quilt. Press.

3. Refer to steps 1 and 2 to join, measure, trim, and sew 1¼"-wide Second Border, 2½"-wide Third Border, and 6"-wide Outside Border strips to top, bottom, and sides of quilt. Press.

LAYERING AND FINISHING

1. Cut backing crosswise into three equal pieces. Sew pieces together lengthwise to make one 84" x 120" (approximate) backing piece. Press and trim to 84" x 94".

2. Referring to Layering the Quilt on page 94, arrange and baste backing, batting and top together. Hand or machine quilt as desired.

3. Refer to Binding the Quilt on page 94. Sew 2¾" x 42" binding strips end-to-end to make one continuous 2¾"-wide binding strip. Bind quilt to finish.

Joy Banner

GETTING STARTED

This banner will shout "Joy" to all who enter your home. The project incorporates wool, appliqués, beading, and embroidery. WoolFelt™ was used throughout this project. To add fullness and texture, refer to Tips for Felting Wool on page 95. Read all instructions before beginning.

MAKING THE BANNER

Refer to appliqué instructions on page 93. Our instructions are for Quick-Fuse Appliqué, but if you prefer hand appliqué, reverse templates, add ¼"-wide seam allowance, and use cotton fabric in place of wool.

1. Use patterns on pages 82, 84, and 85 to trace one of each letter, leaf center and leaf shadow; and one of each poinsettia and shadow on paper side of fusible web. Use appropriate fabrics to prepare all appliqués for fusing.

2. Press 1" x 18½" lightweight fusible web piece to wool strip for stem. Cut a ⅜" x 18" stem strip that will be fused to banner in a gentle curve.

3. Using pinking shears or rotary cutter with a scallop blade, cut 21¾" x 28" Fabric A edges to add interest to banner sides and bottom edges.

4. Refer to photo to position and fuse all appliqués to 19" x 20½" Fabric B piece. Trim stem to desired length prior to fusing. Finish appliqué edges with decorative stitching as desired. We used a machine blanket stitch and gold metallic thread to stitch all letter edges and a green thread for poinsettia shadow, leaf and stem. Poinsettia edges were left free of stitches.

Patterns are reversed for use with Quick-Fuse Applique (page 93)

Tracing Line ——————
Embroidery Placement ·················
(repeat for all petals)

Bead Placement ●

Small Poinsettia Appliqué Pattern

Welcome holiday guests with a joyful greeting on a pretty wool banner on the front door. Bells, beads, and embroidery spread the cheer.

JOY Banner
Finished Size: 21¾" x 25"

5. Refer to Embroidery Stitch Guide on page 95, Poinsettia Appliqué patterns on pages 82 and 84 and photo. Using three strands of gold metallic embroidery floss and a fly stitch, stitch four to five stitches per petal through all layers. Add a bead at point of each fly stitch and secure thread to the back of banner. Referring to photo, stitch and secure additional beads to center of each flower and leaf.

6. Place one 1" x 19" Fabric C strip along top edge behind Banner piece allowing ½" to extend past banner edge. Stitch in place. Repeat for bottom of banner.

7. Referring to photo, stitch gold trim to banner.

8. Fold one 21¾" Fabric A edge under 3" and stitch in place to form rod pocket. Center banner on Fabric A background piece placing top edge 1½" below folded edge. Stitch banner top edge in place.
Tip: We gently lifted banner top edge away from accent strip and stitched through accent piece only which allowed the banner to hide stitch line.

9. Referring to photo, arrange and stitch seven jingle bells to bottom edge of banner.

Large Poinsettia and Shadow
Appliqué Pattern

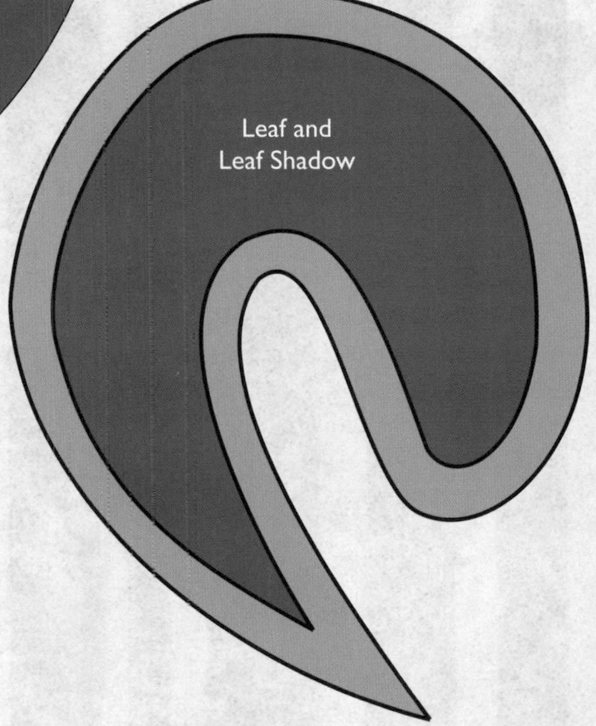

Leaf and
Leaf Shadow

Joy Barner Patterns

Patterns are reversed for use
with Quick-Fuse Applique (page 93)

Tracing Line _____
Embroidery Placement ....
(repeat for all petals)

Bead Placement ●

Debbie's DECORATING TIPS

Beautiful Botanicals

Certain plants have become a traditional part of holiday decorating, and it is always fun to find new ways to use these traditional elements. In my own home, I love decorating with fresh plants for any season, and a rosemary tree, poinsettias, amaryllis, and paperwhite narcissus are often part of my holiday décor.

OLD WORLD SANTA Candleholders

MAKING THE CANDLEHOLDERS

1. Cut balusters to lengths desired. Referring to photo for inspiration, pair balusters with pre-cut rounds or squares as desired. Drill pilot holes and use screws to secure wood pieces. Sand as needed and remove residue.

2. Paint with Light Buttermilk paint. Two or more coats of paint may be needed for good coverage. Allow to dry.

3. Referring to photo for inspiration, select areas on the candlesticks for gold highlights. Following manufacturer's directions, dab gold leaf adhesive on those areas and allow to "set" as directed. Apply gold leaf to adhesive areas, brushing away excess with a soft paintbrush.

4. Lightly sand to soften gold leaf areas.

5. Spray candlesticks with matte varnish and allow to dry.

6. Following manufacturer's directions, apply antiquing medium. Use a rag to rub off antiquing until desired look is achieved

YOU WILL NEED...

- **RECYCLED OR NEW BALUSTERS**
- **PRE-CUT, UNFINISHED WOODEN ROUNDS AND SQUARES** - Variety of Sizes
- **AMERICANA® ACRYLIC CRAFT PAINT** - Light Buttermilk
- **MATTE SPRAY VARNISH**
- **ANTIQUING MEDIUM**
- **SANDPAPER & PAINTBRUSHES**
- **GOLD LEAF & ADHESIVE**
- **DECOUPAGE MEDIUM**
- **DECOART® TWINKLES® WRITER** - Gold
- **PAPER SANTAS OR OTHER DESIGNS FROM NON-COPYRIGHTED SOURCES**
- **WOOD SCREWS**

7. Carefully cut out Santas or other holiday motifs and apply to candlesticks as desired using decoupage medium and following manufacturer's directions. Allow to dry.

8. Coat entire candlestick with another coat or two of decoupage, allowing to dry between coats.

9. Use Twinkles® Writer to add gold glitter highlights as desired.

Dress a rosemary tree up for the holidays with a couple of clever tricks. Create a colorful and interesting pedestal for the plant by turning the saucer upside down and adding a shallow wicker basket in Christmas red color. Continue the red accents, by placing faux berries around the base of the rosemary tree. The effect is interesting and eye-catching. Be very careful watering the plant, though, since the saucer is serving as a pedestal!

Enclose a small poinsettia in a terrarium or vintage birdcage for a fun, fresh look. My glass terrarium is heavy and hard to store, so I Christmas-ize it with a poinsettia and a bead garland so it can remain on display all through the year.

Turn cast-offs into collectibles by making these decorative candleholders. Salvaged sections from an old bed frame were the inspiration for these clever candleholders.

ELEGANT Table Topper

Elegant Table Topper	FIRST CUT		SECOND CUT	
Finished Size: 36" Square	Number of Strips or Pieces	Dimensions	Number of Pieces	Dimensions
Fabric A Block Background ¼ yard	1	5½" x 42"	2	5½" squares
			4	4½" squares
Fabric B Star & Outside Border ⅞ yard	4	6½" x 42"	2	6½" x 36½" (Border)
			2	6½" x 24½" (Border)
			2	5½" squares
			1	4½" square
Fabric C Prairie Points ⅙ yard	1	4½" x 42"	4	4½" squares
BORDERS				
First Border ¼ yard	2	3½" x 42"	2	3½" x 18½"
			2	3½" x 12½"
Mock Piping ⅙ yard	2	1¾" x 42"	4	1¾" x 18½"
Second Border ⅛ yard	2	1½" x 42"	2	1½" x 20½"
			2	1½" x 18½"
Third Border ¼ yard	4	1½" x 42"	2	1½" x 22½"
			2	1½" x 20½"
Fourth Border ¼ yard	4	1½" x 42"	2	1½" x 24½"
			2	1½" x 22½"
Backing - 1⅛ yards				

FABRIC REQUIREMENTS AND CUTTING INSTRUCTIONS

Read all instructions before beginning and use ¼"-wide seam allowance throughout. Read Cutting Strips and Pieces on page 92 prior to cutting fabric.

GETTING STARTED

Elegant, yet simple, describes this 36" square table topper – a great way to finish any room decor. Refer to Accurate Seam Allowance on page 92. Whenever possible use the Assembly Line Method on page 92. Press seams in the direction of arrows. No batting was used so topper lays flat.

MAKING THE TABLE TOPPER

1. Make Half-Square Triangles by drawing a diagonal line on wrong side of one 5½" Fabric A square. Place marked square and one 5½" Fabric B square right side together. Sew a scant ¼" away from drawn line on both sides as shown. Cut on drawn line and press. Make two. This will make four half-square triangle units.

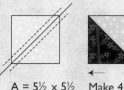

A = 5½ x 5½
B = 5½ x 5½
Make 2

Make 4

2. Make quarter square triangles by drawing a diagonal line on wrong side of one unit from step 1 in opposite direction from seam as shown. Layer two units from step 1, right sides together, placing Fabric A triangle on Fabric B triangle. Sew a scant ¼" away from drawn line on both sides, cut on drawn line, and press. Square unit to 4½". Make two. This will make four quarter square triangles.

Make 4
Square to 4½

3. Sew one unit from step 2 between two 4½" Fabric A squares as shown. Press. Make two.

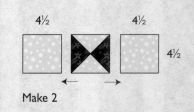

4½ 4½ 4½

Make 2

4. Sew one 4½" Fabric B square between two units from step 2 as shown. Press.

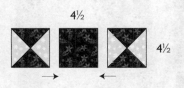

5. Sew unit from step 4 between two units from step 3 as shown. Press. Block measures 12½" square.

Block measures 12½" square

6. Fold and press one 4½" Fabric C square in half diagonally, wrong sides together. Fold and press diagonally in half again, as shown, to make Prairie Point. Raw edges will be together. Make four.

7. Align and center one Prairie Point at center of each outside edge of unit from step 5 with folded edges pointing toward center, and raw edges matching, as shown. Pin or baste in place.

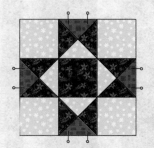

Showcase your favorite holiday fabrics with this easy-to-make table topper. Prairie Points accent the center block and rows of borders add elegant charm.

8. Sew two 3½" x 12½" First Border strips to top and bottom of unit from step 7 as shown, keeping Prairie Points in previous position. Press seam and Prairie Points away from center. Sew two 3½" x 18½" First Border strips to sides of unit. Press. **Optional:** If desired, tack ends of Prairie Points into position to secure.

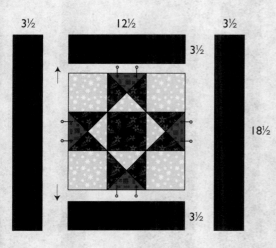

9. Fold four 1¾" x 18½" Mock Piping strips in half lengthwise, wrong sides together. Place on top and bottom of unit from step 8 with folded edge toward center and matching raw edges. Baste in place. Place remaining piping strips on side of unit overlapping previous strips. Baste in place.

10. Sew two 1½" x 18½" Second Border strips to top and bottom of unit from step 9. Press seams towards borders. Sew two 1½" x 20½" Second Border strips to sides. Press.

11. Sew two 1½" x 20½" Third Border strips to top and bottom of unit from step 10. Press. Sew two 1½" x 22½" Third Border strips to sides. Press.

12. Sew two 1½" x 22½" Fourth Border strips to top and bottom of unit from step 11. Press. Sew two 1½" x 24½" Fourth Border strips to sides. Press.

13. Sew two 6½" x 24½" Fabric B strips to top and bottom of unit from step 12. Press. Sew two 6½" x 36½" Fabric B strips to sides. Press.

FINISHING THE TOPPER

Layer and center quilt and 40" x 40" (approximate) backing piece right sides together. Using ¼"-wide seam, stitch around all edges, leaving a 6" opening on one side for turning. Trim backing even with quilt. Clip corners, turn, and press. Hand-stitch opening closed. "Stitch in the ditch" along outside border seam and center block seam to secure layers.

ELEGANT Table Topper
Finished Size: 36" x 36"

GILDED LEAF Tree

This beautiful golden tree will add a touch of elegance to any room and it is surprisingly simple to make!

MAKING THE LEAF TREE

Spray cone with bronze or gold paint and allow to dry. Beginning at the bottom, use low temperature hot glue to fasten a row of leaves around bottom of cone, overlapping leaves slightly.

Move up the cone to fasten another row of leaves, overlapping the first row by about an inch. Glue only at the top of each leaf, leaving the bottom edge free.

Continue gluing leaves in rows. At the narrow part of the tree, use straight pins to hold sides of the leaves to the cone shape. When all of cone is covered with leaves, form a bow using the sheer ribbon and wire. Glue to the top of the tree.

YOU WILL NEED...

- **24" STYROFOAM® CONE**
- **SEVERAL SPRAYS OF GOLD-COLORED LEAVES**
  (Check the floral dept at craft and discount stores. Our leaves are an average of 3½" long and 1¼" wide.)
- **GLUE GUN & LOW TEMPERATURE GLUE STICKS**
- **SMALL STRAIGHT PINS**
- **BRONZE OR GOLD ACRYLIC SPRAY PAINT**
- **¾" SHEER RIBBON TO MATCH LEAVES**
- **CRAFT WIRE**
- **ASSORTED PAINTBRUSHES**

Debbie's DECORATING TIPS

Holiday Reflections

Reflect the bright sentiments and brilliant joys of the holidays in your home décor by using mirrors and shiny surfaces as part of your decorating scheme. Elegant and eye-catching, these decorating ideas make great focal points.

A glass bowl at once shows off tiny treasures and reflects the light in this beautiful side table display. Crystal beads around the rim pick up the candlelight and silver treasures in the bowl add even more gleaming light. Faux snow grounds the centerpiece and helps soften the shine.

A square tray is fitted with a mirror and surrounded with shiny silver beads for a spectacular coffee table centerpiece. Glass candlesticks and a sparkly finish on the candles add to the radiant reflective quality of this timeless decoration.

GENERAL Directions

CUTTING STRIPS & PIECES

We recommend washing cotton fabrics in cold water and pressing before making projects in this book. Using a rotary cutter, see-through ruler, and a cutting mat, cut the strips and pieces for the project. If indicated on the Cutting Chart, some will need to be cut again into smaller strips and pieces. Make second cuts in order shown to maximize use of fabric. The yardage amounts and cutting instructions are based on an approximate fabric width of 42".

FUSSY CUT

To make a "fussy cut," carefully position ruler or template over a selected design in fabric. Include seam allowances before cutting desired pieces.

ASSEMBLY LINE METHOD

Whenever possible, use an assembly line method. Position pieces right sides together and line up next to sewing machine. Stitch first unit together, then continue sewing others without breaking threads. When all units are sewn, clip threads to separate. Press seams in the direction of arrows.

ACCURATE SEAM ALLOWANCE

Accurate seam allowances are always important, but especially when the blocks contain many pieces and the quilt top contains multiple pieced borders. If each seam is off as little as $\frac{1}{16}$", you'll soon find yourself struggling with components that just won't fit.

To ensure seams are a perfect $\frac{1}{4}$"-wide, try this simple test: Cut three strips of fabric, each exactly $1\frac{1}{2}$" x 12". With right sides together, and long raw edges aligned, sew two strips together, carefully maintaining a $\frac{1}{4}$" seam. Press seam to one side. Add the third strip to complete the strip set. Press and measure. The finished strip set should measure $3\frac{1}{2}$" x 12". The center strip should measure 1"-wide, the two outside strips $1\frac{1}{4}$"-wide, and the seam allowances exactly $\frac{1}{4}$".

If your measurements differ, check to make sure that seams have been pressed flat. If strip set still doesn't "measure up," try stitching a new strip set, adjusting the seam allowance until a perfect $\frac{1}{4}$"-wide seam is achieve.

PRESSING

Pressing is very important for accurate seam allowances. Press seams using either steam or dry heat with an "up and down" motion. Do not use side-to-side motion as this will distort the unit or block. Set the seam by pressing along the line of stitching, then press seams to one side as indicated by project instructions and diagram arrows.

QUICK CORNER TRIANGLES

Quick corner triangles are formed by simply sewing fabric squares to other squares or rectangles. The directions and diagrams with each project illustrate what size pieces to use and where to place squares on the corresponding piece. Follow steps 1–3 below to make quick corner triangle units.

1. With pencil and ruler, draw diagonal line on wrong side of fabric square that will form the triangle. This will be your sewing line.

Sewing line

2. With right sides together, place square on corresponding piece. Matching raw edges, pin in place, and sew ON drawn line. Trim off excess fabric, leaving $\frac{1}{4}$"-wide seam allowance as shown.

Trim $\frac{1}{4}$" away from sewing line

3. Press seam in direction of arrow as shown in step-by-step project diagram. Measure completed quick corner triangle unit to ensure the greatest accuracy.

Finished quick corner triangle unit

Quick-Fuse Appliqué

Quick-fuse appliqué is a method of adhering appliqué pieces to a background with fusible web. For quick and easy results, simply quick-fuse appliqué pieces in place. Use sewable, lightweight fusible web for the projects in this book unless otherwise indicated. Finish raw edges with stitching as desired. Laundering is not recommended unless edges are finished.

1. With paper side up, lay fusible web over appliqué pattern. Leaving ½" space between pieces, trace all elements of design. Cut around traced pieces, approximately ¼" outside traced line.

fusible web

2. With paper side up, position and press fusible web to wrong side of selected fabrics. Follow manufacturer's directions for iron temperature and fusing time. Cut out each piece on traced line.

fabric-wrong side

3. Remove paper backing from pieces. A thin film will remain on wrong side of fabric. Position and fuse all pieces of one appliqué design at a time onto background, referring to photos for placement. Fused design will be the reverse of traced pattern.

Appliqué Pressing Sheet

An appliqué pressing sheet is very helpful when there are many small elements to apply using a quick-fuse appliqué technique. The pressing sheet allows small items to be bonded together before applying them to the background. The sheet is coated with a special material that prevents fusible web from adhering permanently to the sheet. Follow manufacturer's directions. Remember to let fabric cool completely before lifting it from the appliqué sheet. If not cooled, the fusible web could remain on the sheet instead of on the fabric.

Machine Appliqué

This technique should be used when you are planning to launder quick-fuse projects. Several different stitches can be used: small narrow zigzag stitch, satin stitch, blanket stitch, or another decorative machine stitch. Use an open toe appliqué foot if your machine has one. Use a stabilizer to obtain even stitches and help prevent puckering. Always practice first to check machine settings.

1. Fuse all pieces following Quick-Fuse Appliqué directions.

2. Cut a piece of stabilizer large enough to extend beyond the area to be stitched. Pin to the wrong side of fabric.

3. Select thread to match appliqué.

4. Following the order that appliqués were positioned, stitch along the edges of each section. Anchor beginning and ending stitches by tying off or stitching in place two or three times.

5. Complete all stitching, then remove stabilizer.

Hand Appliqué

Hand appliqué is easy when you start out with the right supplies. Cotton and machine embroidery thread are easy to work with. Pick a color that matches the appliqué fabric as closely as possible. Use appliqué or silk pins for holding shapes in place and a long, thin needle, such as a sharp, for stitching.

1. Make a template for every shape in the appliqué design. Use a dotted line to show where pieces overlap.

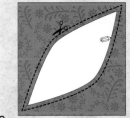

2. Place template on right side of appliqué fabric. Trace around template.

3. Cut out shapes ¼" beyond traced line.

4. Position shapes on background fabric, referring to quilt layout. Pin shapes in place.

5. When layering and stitching appliqué shapes, always work from background to foreground. Where shapes overlap, do not turn under and stitch edges of bottom pieces. Turn and stitch the edges of the piece on top.

6. Use the traced line as your turn-under guide. Entering from the wrong side of the appliqué shape, bring the needle up on the traced line. Using the tip of the needle, turn under the fabric along the traced line. Using blind stitch, stitch along folded edge to join the appliqué shape to the background fabric. Turn under and stitch about ¼" at a time.

ADDING THE BORDERS

1. Measure quilt through the center from side to side. Trim two border strips to this measurement. Sew to top and bottom of quilt. Press seams toward border.

2. Measure quilt through the center from top to bottom, including borders added in step 1. Trim border strips to this measurement. Sew to sides and press. Repeat to add additional borders.

MITERED BORDERS

A mitered border is usually "fussy cut" to highlight a motif or design. Borders are cut slightly longer than needed to allow for centering of motif or matching corners.

1. Cut the border strips or strip sets as indicated for quilt.

2. Measure each side of the quilt and mark center with a pin. Fold each border strip in half crosswise to find its midpoint and mark with a pin. Using the side measurements, measure out from the midpoint and place a pin to show where the edges of the quilt will be.

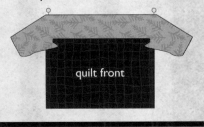

midpoint

3. Align a border strip to quilt. Pin at midpoints and pin-marked ends first, then along entire side, easing to fit if necessary.

4. Sew border to quilt, stopping and starting ¼" from pin-marked end points. Repeat to sew all four border strips to quilt.

quilt front

5. Fold corner of quilt diagonally, right sides together, matching seams and borders. Place a long ruler along fold line extending across border. Draw a diagonal line across border from fold to edge of border. This is the stitching line. Starting at ¼" mark, stitch on drawn line. Check for squareness, then trim excess. Press seam open.

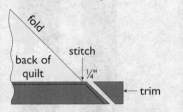

fold

back of quilt

stitch

¼"

← trim

LAYERING THE QUILT

1. Cut backing and batting 4" to 8" larger than quilt top.

2. Lay pressed backing on bottom (right side down), batting in middle, and pressed quilt top (right side up) on top. Make sure everything is centered and that backing and batting are flat. Backing and batting will extend beyond quilt top.

3. Begin basting in center and work toward outside edges. Baste vertically and horizontally, forming a 3"–4" grid. Baste or pin completely around edge of quilt top. Quilt as desired. Remove basting.

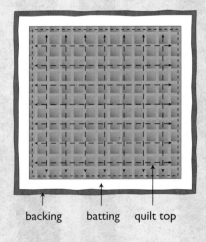

backing   batting   quilt top

BINDING THE QUILT

1. Trim batting and backing to ¼" beyond raw edge of quilt top. This will add fullness to binding.

2. Join binding strips to make one continuous strip if needed. To join, place strips perpendicular to each other, right sides together, and draw a line. Sew on drawn line and trim triangle extensions, leaving a ¼"-wide seam allowance. Continue stitching ends together to make the desired length. Press seams open.

←trim

3. Fold and press binding strips in half lengthwise with wrong sides together.

4. Measure quilt through center from side to side. Cut two binding strips to this measurement. Lay binding strips on top and bottom edges of quilt top with raw edges of binding and quilt top aligned. Sew through all layers, ¼" from quilt edge. Press binding away from quilt top.

Front of Quilt

5. Measure quilt through center from top to bottom, including binding just added. Cut two binding strips to this measurement and sew to sides through all layers, including binding just added. Press.

6. Folding top and bottom first, fold binding around to back then repeat with sides. Press and pin in position. Hand-stitch binding in place using a blind stitch.

←fold
top and bottom binding in first

FINISHING PILLOWS

1. Layer batting between pillow top and lining. Baste. Hand or machine quilt as desired, unless otherwise indicated. Trim batting and lining even with raw edge of pillow top.

2. Narrow hem one long edge of each backing piece by folding under ¼" to wrong side. Press. Fold under ¼" again to wrong side. Press. Stitch along folded edge.

3. With right sides up, lay one backing piece over second piece so hemmed edges overlap, making backing unit the same measurement as the pillow top. Baste backing pieces together at top and bottom where they overlap.

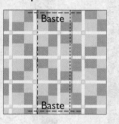

4. With right sides together, position and pin pillow top to backing. Using ¼"-wide seam, sew around edges, trim corners, turn right side out, and press.

PILLOW FORMS

Cut two pieces of fabric to finished size of pillow form plus ½". Place right sides together, aligning raw edges. Using ¼"-wide seam, sew around all edges, leaving 4" opening for turning. Trim corners and turn right side out. Stuff to desired fullness with polyester fiberfill and hand-stitch opening closed.

TIPS FOR FELTING WOOL

1. Plunge wool fabric in boiling water for 5 minutes then plunge it into icy water until very chilled. Do not mix colors as dyes may run.

2. Blot wool with a dry towel and place both towel and wool in dryer on high heat until thoroughly dry. The result is a thicker, fuller fabric that will give added texture to the wool. Pressing felted wool is not recommended, as it will flatten the texture. Most wools will shrink 10-15% when boiled, adjust yardage accordingly.

COUCHING TECHNIQUE

Couching is a method of attaching a textured yarn, cord, or fiber to fabric for decorative purposes. Use an open-toe embroidery foot, couching foot, or a zigzag presser foot and matching or monofilament thread. Sew with a long zigzag stitch just barely wider than the cord or yarn. Stabilizer on the wrong side of fabric is recommended. Place the yarn, cord, or fiber on right side of fabric and zigzag to attach as shown. A hand-stitch can be used if desired.

Couching

GENERAL PAINTING DIRECTIONS

Read all instructions on paint products before using and carefully follow manufacturer's instructions and warnings. For best results, allow paint to dry thoroughly between each coat and between processes unless directed otherwise. Wear face mask and safety goggles when sanding. Rubber gloves are recommended when handling stains and other finishing products.

EMBROIDERY STITCH GUIDE

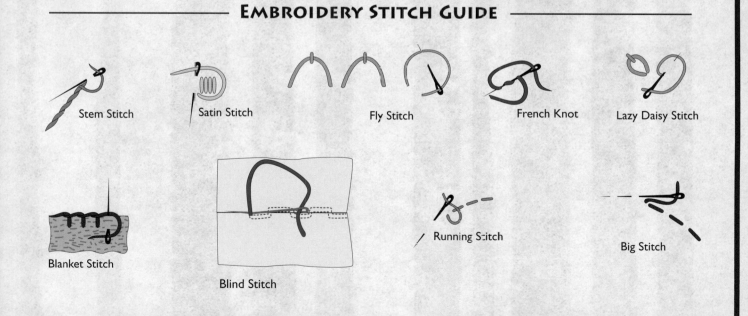

Stem Stitch Satin Stitch Fly Stitch French Knot Lazy Daisy Stitch

Blanket Stitch Blind Stitch Running Stitch Big Stitch

ABOUT Debbie Mumm

A talented designer, author, and entrepreneur, Debbie Mumm has been creating charming artwork and quilt designs for more than twenty year

Debbie got her start in the quilting industry in 1986 with her unique and simple-to-construct quilt patterns. Since that time, she has authored more than fifty book featuring quilting and home decorating projects ar has led her business to become a multi-faceted enterprise that includes publishing, fabric design, and licensed art divisions.

Known world-wide for the many licensed products that feature her designs, Debbie loves to bring traditional elements together with fresh palettes and modern themes to create the look of today's country.

DESIGNS BY DEBBIE MUMM
Special thanks to my creative teams:

EDITORIAL & PROJECT DESIGN
Carolyn Ogden: Publications & Marketing Manager
Nancy Kirkland: Seamstress/Quilter • Georgie Gerl: Technical Writer/Editor
Carolyn Lowe: Technical Editor • Jackie Saling: Craft Designer
Anita Pederson: Machine Quilter

BOOK DESIGN & PRODUCTION
Tom Harlow: Graphics Manager • Monica Ziegler: Graphic Designer
Kristi Somday: Graphic Designer
Kathy Rickel: Art Studio Assistant • Kris Clifford: Executive Assistant

PHOTOGRAPHY
Debbie Mumm® Graphics Studio

ART TEAM
Kathy Arbuckle: Artist/Designer • Gil-Jin Foster: Artist

The Debbie Mumm® Sewing Studio exclusively uses Bernina® sewing machines.
©2007 Debbie Mumm

Discover More from Debbie Mumm®

Debbie Mumm's®
Greenwood Gardens
96-page, soft cover

Debbie Mumm's®
New Expressions
96-page, soft cover

Memories & Milestones
by Debbie Mumm®
96-page, soft cover

Seasons
by Debbie Mumm®
96-page, soft cover

PRODUCED BY:
Debbie Mumm, Inc.
1116 E. Westview Court
Spokane, WA 99218
(509) 466-3572
Fax (509) 466-6919

www.debbiemumm.com

PUBLISHED BY:
Leisure Arts, Inc
5701 Ranch Drive
Little Rock, AR • 72223
www.leisurearts.com

Available at local fabric and craft shops or at
debbiemumm.com